ADVANCE PRAISE

"*Great Networking* is more than just a 'practical tips' guide to networking events. Alisa Grafton takes a thoughtful approach to networking and building professional relationships that provides the platform to give the tips she shares better context and makes them easier to apply. An excellent read."

ANDY LOPATA, International speaker, podcast host and author of five books on networking and professional relationships

"Alisa cleverly reveals in this brilliant guide that the secret to successful networking is to enjoy it. What better way to learn how to do this than by hearing from those who have taken that journey themselves? The invaluable knowledge in these pages gleaned from so many experts is itself a masterclass in networking by Alisa."

RICHARD MACKLIN, Former Global Client Partner, Dentons and Director, FulfilledLeaders.com

"Alisa Grafton offers even the most reluctant networkers a contemporary guide into both the 'why' and 'how' of networking today."

MAYA GUDKA, Executive Coach and author,
London Business School

"Having led the media project ZIMA and the fund Gift of Life – both of which are at the centre of the Russian immigrants' community in London – for the last few years, I have learned that relationships between people are at the heart of literally everything. Not everyone finds it easy and natural to build relationships, especially the professional kind, so *Great Networking* carries special value. It will help people to feel happier in life generally."

LYUBA GALKINA, Trustee of Gift of Life,
co-founder of the ZIMA group, former senior marketer at Pepsi, Nike, Apple and Google

"Alisa shows that being a great networker is essentially the same as being a person that others want to be around. She demystifies the topic, brings new insight and sheds light on things we probably know intuitively about natural networkers. It's an engaging and thoroughly enjoyable read. I'd recommend it to anyone who is interested in connecting with other humans in an engaging and genuine way."

SALLY BIBB, Founding Director of Engaging Minds
and author of *The Strengths Book*

"Our advocates and personal network are key to career development. They are often the SOLE source of a future role. *Great Networking* is a valuable guide because it is so highly practical, and rightly emphasizes some often under-played factors – such as authenticity, sheer likeability, and how to build your network even if you see yourself as an introvert."

MAX LANDSBERG, Author of bestselling *The Tao of Coaching*

"*Great Networking* turns what is often seen as cringeworthy and done ineffectively into a rewarding and mutually satisfying personal and professional practice. From cultivating the right mindset to developing skills such as meaningful conversations and maintaining your network, this book by Alisa Grafton is packed with 'real world' advice that will ensure your success."

STEVEN D'SOUZA, Senior Client Partner, Korn Ferry, author of *Brilliant Networking* and co-author of the award-winning *Not Knowing* trilogy

Published by
LID Publishing
An imprint of LID Business Media Ltd.
The Record Hall, Studio 304,
16-16a Baldwins Gardens,
London EC1N 7RJ, UK

info@lidpublishing.com
www.lidpublishing.com

A member of:

BPR ⊛

businesspublishersroundtable.com

© Alisa Grafton, 2022
© LID Business Media Limited, 2022

Printed by Severn, Gloucester
ISBN: 978-1-911671-95-4
ISBN: 978-1-911671-96-1 (ebook)

Cover and page design: Caroline Li

ALISA GRAFTON

GREAT
NETWORKING

THE ART AND PRACTICE
OF BUILDING AUTHENTIC
PROFESSIONAL RELATIONSHIPS

MADRID | MEXICO CITY | LONDON
NEW YORK | BUENOS AIRES
BOGOTA | SHANGHAI | NEW DELHI

CONTENTS

Acknowledgements   1

PART 1:
THE ART OF RELATIONSHIP BUILDING

1. Relationships in the professional world   8

2. Why does it feel so scary to network?   16

3. Networking's bad rep   26

4. My story of failures (it happens to the best of us)   32

5. What 'great' looks like: authentic people build
authentic relationships   40

6. We are meant to connect, naturally   54

7. Your social capital   64

8. The problem with disconnection and social anxiety:
how being compassionate to oneself can help   74

9. The biggest secret is... know your purpose   82

10. Be a giver, but not a selfless kind   92

PART 2:
THE HOWS OF WORKING ANY ROOM

11. A shared playground for everyone   102

12. What if I am an introvert?
(And other superpowers)   110

13. The most important rules of networking:
how to read the room and speak
to anyone with ease and grace   120

14. Small talk versus meaningful conversations   132

15. Curiouser and curiouser   146

16. Being vulnerable in order to be connected   156

17. Getting over the awkward and the scary:
the less-pretty faces of networking and
the power of the fear of rejection   162

18. How to end a conversation gracefully   172

19. The art and the lessons of virtual networking   178

PART 3:
REAP JOY AND MUTUAL BENEFITS
FROM BEING CONNECTED

20. This relationship is a marathon, not a sprint   186

21. Wisdom for ambitious networkers   194

Endnotes   203

About the author   207

The blurb   208

TO MY MOTHER MARINA,
WHO HAS TAUGHT ME THAT
RELATIONSHIPS ARE EVERYTHING,

AND TO MY DAUGHTER ROMY,
WHO SEEMS TO KNOW THIS ALREADY.

ACKNOWLEDGEMENTS

This is my favourite part of the book. The relationships that we form, nurture and enjoy have a magical quality to them – they inspire us, challenge us, support us, put us back together when we fall apart, show us the way, make us do some much-needed thinking, embrace us and add an enormous amount of joy to our life.

No man is an island.

And so, this book is not only about relationship-building, it's also the *result* of the relationships that I am lucky to have in my life. My journey would not have led me to the point where this book would have been in existence were it not for the people that this part is all about.

Some time ago, when Bob Ferguson suggested that I write a book on networking, I thought he was mad. But Bob clearly explained exactly why he was not, and why the daunting task of writing while holding down a full-time job was within my reach. Thank you, Bob. You were right, and I was wrong.

About the job – writing this book would have been a considerably more arduous process without the support of my partners at De Pinna LLP.

David, Martin B, Phillip, Sebastian, Martin C, Ryan, Peter, Siôn and Sara – your enthusiasm, your interest in the book and your belief in me have been critical in making it happen. My journey as a first-time writer would have been a lot harder without your backing. I'm lucky to have you as my partners. Thank you.

I am very grateful to my colleagues at De Pinna, past and present, who have been sharing their thoughts and opinions on professional relationships with me, and for all your fabulous enthusiasm for the book. Narmina, Sina, Kalina, Fanny, Peggah, Emily, Patrick and Armin, to name but a few. You have been an inspiration, and you each have so much going for you! Iain, thank you for your precious friendship spanning the last 20 years. Finally, a shout out to Karleen for her eagle-eyed attention and well-timed insight.

Alec Egan – thank you for the hours spent talking about the projects, for your recommendations of great authors to read and for opening to me the world of LID Publishing.

Martin Liu, what a welcoming and supportive world it is! Thank you for making me feel like a part of the family from the start, for being such a positive rainmaker and for your faith in the book.

My editor at LID, Aiyana Curtis, has made light work of what I feared to be the hardest part of the book – the writing process. Thank you, Aiyana, for your encouragement, for your helpful attitude and for your ultimate professionalism!

There is a special skill in separating linguistic debris from genuine author's voice, and for this I am grateful to Brian Doyle, and to Bella Sophia for her unique attention to detail.

Caroline Li – thank you for your creative vision and for bringing into life this stunning design.

The usefulness of a book stretches beyond a collection of sensible words wrapped in a beautiful cover, and my thanks are to Teya Ucherdzhieva for helping to connect my reader with my work.

When the decision to write this book was formed, I reached out to those that I had observed over the years to masterfully build great professional relationships around them. I called them Master Networkers. Most of them insisted that there was no mastery in their relationship-building styles, which has only reconfirmed my view!

Sue Langley, John Nicolson, Elizabeth Filippouli, Clare Murray, Trevor Barton, Ben Wells, Artem Doudko,

Lyuba Galkina, Kevin Rogers, Richard Macklin, Humphrey Douglas, Anita Hoffmann and Phillip Journeaux – I can safely say that without your example, this book would not exist. At different stages of my professional life, each of you have had a major impact in developing my thinking on what it means to be good at building relationships. Master Networkers – I am very grateful to each of you for your input into this book.

My close friends, I would be the shell of a person without you! Natalia, Elena and Neil, Paddy, Olga, Wolfgang – your care and belief in me are humbling.

Sergei Ostrovsky, Dr Natalia Mosunova, Alexander Khvoshchinskiy, Lisa Williams, Alex Green and Sophy Copland – our conversations at the right time have had a profound effect on me. Thank you for sharing your wisdom with me.

Andy Lopata – thank you for your generosity and for your insight. I'm in awe of the way you back your inspiring ideas with meaningful action.

When you are a mum to a young child, writing a book feels like carving out the time for writing with a plastic knife. It's tricky. Thank you to our nanny, Janice Hughes, for giving me the peace of mind when I need it; it's priceless.

And finally, to my husband Phil – you rock. The most challenging but also the most rewarding and enriching relationships are those we have with the people closest to us. This book would not have been written in six months of weekend and evening work had it not been for your selfless help. Thank you very much for your unabated faith in me, and for your generosity of spirit in always encouraging me to do what I believe in, and to do it well. And for making me laugh when it matters the most.

PART 1

THE ART OF RELATIONSHIP BUILDING

1

RELATIONSHIPS IN THE PROFESSIONAL WORLD

I began writing this book in 2021, a year into the global COVID-19 pandemic... time that has become an eye-opener for many of us. Some may have realized that their priorities were not in the right order, whilst others were becoming increasingly aware of how much the relationships in their lives affected their contentment and, really, most aspects of their wellbeing.

Multiple studies have concluded that the key to happiness is the quality of the relationships that we have in life. In turn, honest, candid communication is the cornerstone of being fulfilled in those relationships that are built on mutual trust and respect. It is hard to imagine a fulfilling, enriching relationship where people are not aware or respectful of each other's principal values and priorities. As much as we all have individual needs and wants, most of us are united by one powerful desire. This boils down to something my best friend said to me many years ago, and it has become my guiding star. "We all want to be understood," she mused, and the mighty simplicity of this notion has stuck.

It is easy to see the value of strong relationships and good communication in our private lives. Yet, somehow, this does not seem to translate easily into the professional environment. It's not unusual to believe that dedication to your job alone is what determines future success, with the relationship factor taking a supporting role. However much we may wish to separate 'life' and 'work,' the latter is merely a different setting for continuing the former. Hence, all the usual life rules apply, including the one about all of us wanting to be understood, and to be a part of something bigger than ourselves.

The book you are holding in your hands is not another guide to climbing your career ladder faster. Rather, it is about changing the way we approach building relationships. It's about dialling back to what we, as humans, are meant to do best: weave together the nets of people who support, celebrate and raise each other up.

Writing about networking, I cannot help but note the tension between the term's connotations and its true meaning. What do *you* think of when someone mentions the term 'networking?' A sleazy salesman? Strained small talk in a room full of unfamiliar faces, while nervously clutching a glass of wine?

Or, is it an *opportunity*, first and foremost? Do you think of the potential that a new meeting can bring? Or, perhaps, an absorbing conversation with someone who has an interesting point of view on a subject you care about? Maybe it's much-needed advice on how the person you just met dealt with a professional issue you'd grappled with.

I have found all of the above, and much, much more, in my two decades of networking in the business world of the City of London and beyond. Networking has genuinely transformed the direction my career took, and to this day I continue to greatly benefit from the old and new connections that the exercise of the relationship building – networking – has afforded me.

The term 'social capital' will be referenced more than once in this book. This is because the capital we raise through the social connections we create is very much akin to its financial cousin. The higher the value of your capital, the higher *your* value is. Yet, to be clear, that value does not always align with the social standing of your connections. In the dynamic societies we live in today, social standing is a fluid concept, and your 'investments' should reflect this notion.

While the value of engaging in networking efforts rarely needs to be preached, the precise mechanics of effectively doing so are often shrouded in mystery. In this book, I am looking to demystify the process of forming and reinforcing professional relationships. And, speaking as someone who has lived through most of them, I want to openly address common concerns and worries. It is my goal to candidly share my personal experience, as well as extensive research into what it means to be an effective networker.

One of the most prominent leading experts on business networking, Dr Ivan Misner founded BNI® (Business Network International), the world's largest referral network, in 1985 as a way for business people to connect and make introductions in a structured, professional environment. He has said that "people who concentrate entirely on the material and financial aspects of business fail to realize that, in the end, all business is conducted through personal relationship."[1]

As we will discover in later chapters, this is not just jargon, and the logic behind the sentiment is disarming. We may be complex human beings, laden with the weight of professional qualifications and spurred on by career ambitions, yet feeling safe and secure remains a fundamental need. Consciously or not, this compels us to gravitate towards those who we sense to be trustworthy, who seem to offer a secure space.

'Someone you can trust' remains one of the biggest compliments a person can give or receive. Although it's often mentioned in the professional world, trust doesn't refer to a set of professional qualifications or expert competence. It is merely a reflection of the qualities that engender a feeling of security. Expertise can be learned, but trustworthiness is cultivated. The path to becoming a trustworthy individual is full of seen and unseen obstacles, and walking it well requires awareness of oneself and awareness of those around you. The prize at the end – a reputation for being trustworthy – is like gold dust.

Yet, trust alone, while providing a solid foundation, does not necessarily endear one to others. Trustworthiness is the essential element in relationship building, but it does not make for memorable interactions. It doesn't spark magnetic attraction, create warmth or encourage acceptance. These are driven by another quality that any effective networker will find indispensable: the ability to be liked. The myth seems to be that the 'likeability factor' is something you are either born with or not. One cannot make others like them. Or can they?

Contrary to what we are often told, likeability can be broken down into a set of qualities that can be understood, practiced and acquired, transforming a seemingly charmless individual into one who magnetically draws others in.

Joseph Fuller, Professor of Management Practise at Harvard Business School and co-lead of its Managing the Future of Work initiative, said this of the role of the future manager: "The line, 'Because I said so,' is pretty much extinct."[2] With the changing role of management, employees will also need a different set of skills to be considered for leadership positions. "Those with highly developed social abilities, including the capacity to interact with an unfamiliar person effectively, good listening skills, real-time processing skills," will pull one ahead, says Fuller. "Over time, this keeps gaining share relative to technical skills."

In this book, we will look at how a focus on relationship building – using the fundamental elements of trust and likeability – paves way to professional success. We'll take a practical approach to acquiring the skills and knowledge needed to become memorable, trusted and liked: just the sort of professional and individual people will gravitate to and want to do business with.

As a focus on technology continues to dominate our thinking, it is likely to divert attention from developing our interpersonal skills. Looking a few years ahead, we are more likely to be well versed in the latest tech obsession than intuitively reading the facial expression of the person we're speaking with. The transformative role that virtual communication has played in our life has a dark underbelly: it dulls our essential social instincts. It prevents us from honing the skills necessary for developing social connections, nurturing relationships and, ultimately, taking our rightful place in society. An under-developed ability to connect with others and build relationships will inevitably lead to unfulfilled professional ambitions and an altogether unsatisfying social life.

Artificial Intelligence (AI) is certainly a next step in humankind's progress, but it is sometimes seen as a substitute for human-to-human interaction. It may provide a shortcut to getting things done, but at the expense of addressing the complex elements of basic human nature and interpersonal discourse.

In this book, we are looking to deconstruct the perceived complexity of meeting others and building relationships into easily understood elements, and to throw light on the underlying concepts, which are often shrouded in mystery. Ultimately, whether in personal or professional life, relationships are formed with flesh-and-blood people. Their innermost human needs do not fundamentally change when they transition from home to work. Therefore, the premise of this book is to break down the science and practice of relationship building into bite-size pieces, and use these to form an integrated tapestry of what good – or even *great* – looks like.

WHY DOES IT FEEL SO SCARY TO NETWORK?

If the desire to socialize is inherent to us, why does meeting others often feel like such hard work?

Only the most extroverted among us do not need to prepare mentally to face a roomful of new people, be it online or in person. The vast majority of us can relate to the often-excruciating effort of getting psychologically ready to meet new people. 'Becoming open' is a complex state of mind that requires stepping out of one's comfort zone. A comfort zone is, as the name suggests, a pretty comfy place to inhabit. Think of it as your beloved, well-used sofa, where every bump and fold is familiar, easy to adjust to and perfectly cosy. That familiarity helps alleviate anxiety, so we gravitate there to decompress after a stressful day.

Such a comforting spot is of much value when sanctuary is what we seek. Yet, when we are seeking to establish new contacts, comfort should not be what guides us. Meeting new people tends to take most of us out of our comfort zone. It can make us question who we are, what we stand for, how we are perceived, and whether we're interesting enough, worth being spoken to, would know what to say when there is a pause, and whether we can joke around (and whether our jokes are appropriate). It can make us doubt whether we can cope with rejection, muster enough discipline to pay attention to what our interlocutor is saying, and know when and how to leave, should the conversation go on for too long.

It's no surprise that meeting new people can feel like a whole lot of effort, because it really is!

Indeed, this would be a logical point to end my book – just 19 pages in – if I didn't place so much value on getting out of the comfort zone. The effort you invest in answering all of the 'what ifs' and 'whethers' will be richly rewarded through learning to build relationships. This is such an emotive subject because relationships form the foundation of everything we are as the human race. Consciously or subconsciously, we simply know that there is too much at stake to be careless when it comes to relating to others.

Our ancestral need for being part of a 'tribe' runs deep, and the longing for social approval stems directly from a primitive fear of being ostracized from the social structure we are a part of. A hundred thousand years ago, being rejected by your group spelled certain death. Although we have moved beyond that prospect in stark life or death terms, our psychological need to bond with others and to fit in continues to underlie our actions... as well as stoke our fears.

In the 21st century, the consequences of being rejected by the proverbial tribe may be less dire, but there are factors at play that make the stakes seem just as high.

These go to the reality of leading today's transparent way of life, and the sense of exposure that many find inescapable. The boundaries have become blurred between what is private – what we want to be kept hidden – and what is subject to public scrutiny and discussion. At every turn we can easily anticipate our lives and our interactions being recorded and potentially kept for posterity; our behaviour, reactions, failures and opinions dissected, opined upon and judged by untold numbers of people. The potential of becoming 'cancelled' for saying the wrong thing (by another person's standard), or publicly ridiculed for failing to behave as expected (according to another's criteria), is so real that many choose to stay away from engaging in the circles that are less familiar to them. This is when keeping to your group and staying in your comfort zone feels entirely justified, and even wise.

Yet, I hope that as you journey through this book it becomes convincingly clear that our fears are unfounded. Varying degrees of disapproval and rejection are all very much a part of life. In fact, they're reflective of a life well lived, pursued courageously through daring to embrace the unknown. Being turned down feels painful because it encourages our inner-critic in the dreaded suspicion that we're not good enough. Opening our eyes to this link can provide an effective counterbalance to the fear of being rejected.

As any practiced networker would confess, a withering look from a sought-after business contact can feel like a stab in the heart and make self-doubts resurface like worms on a rainy day. The temptation to turn on yourself in these circumstances can be overwhelming:

we are subconsciously seeking confirmation that the dismissive look was deserving. Was it our manner in approaching the person? Was it something in the way we looked? Was it the colour of our skin, our accent, or maybe the way we were dressed? Was it because we weren't important enough, due to our lowly position, or was our general lack of self-confidence evident a mile away? Was it our socially awkward demeanour, dithering manner, or simply the fact that we are just *unlikeable*? (Ah, the likeability factor! We'll deconstruct and rework this crucial ingredient for any effective networking in Chapter 5.)

Being rejected in the context of a social interaction can encompass many things. It can be as subtle as being interrupted and spoken over. Or, it can be as blunt as being told that someone is unavailable to speak with us. Rejection comes in many guises, but the telltale sign is that sinking feeling when we feel less than welcome where we are. And while niggling self-doubt and sense of not being 'worthy of attention' can sabotage many blossoming interactions, many of us have a reliable radar for the scenarios where we are undervalued. These are the situations when the feeling of being rejected by another person is most likely justified by the actual circumstances, rather than something that we 'imagine.' Even then, however, is it really a worst-case scenario?

Early in my career, while attending a networking event, I spent the first part of the evening pep-talking myself to muster the courage to talk to a senior business person who I believed would be a perfect client for my firm. In my head, I went over my introductory 'elevator pitch' again and again, and applied and reapplied bright lipstick to give myself a psychological boost. I downed a glass of champagne for Dutch courage. I kept discreetly watching my target all evening, waiting for the opportune moment. Finally, I noticed by his body language that, although still engaged in a group conversation, he was ready to talk to someone new. I drew my shoulders back, and with a big smile I walked up to him. Desperate to hide my nerves, I introduced myself in a confidently steady voice and stretched out my hand, ready for a firm handshake. Instead, I received a reluctant 'wet fish' of a shake and a nod that acknowledged my presence... but no more than that. The man did not proceed to give his name or professional affiliation, or volunteer any information whatsoever about himself. He was, quite frankly, *not interested.*

I felt shrunken to the size of a fly, the confidence I'd worked so hard on building up getting the knockout of its life. I proceeded to blabber on about what it was that I did, and why I wanted to talk to him, but it felt exceedingly laborious in the face of zero enthusiasm or interest. I simply hadn't expected that level of dismissal. I wish I could say that I found it in me to turn this lack of interest around, and we became best friends. We did not. In fact, I felt absolutely crushed. I slid away, mumbling something about it being nice to meet him, and spent the rest of the evening (and the following few days) musing on what a total loser I was. Was I really that devoid of social skills and charisma?

The truth is, I was not. A bitter person in me wants to scream that it was, in fact, that self-important blowhard who turned out to be a complete loser with zero social skills. Yet, on reflection, it may well have been that I simply didn't form part of his agenda for that evening. It's quite possible that he felt speaking to me would keep him from meeting others he really wanted to connect with. He chose not to engage, and as a result I was hung out to dry. It was an altogether unpleasant experience for me, even if it helped that person meet his objectives at the time.

It is my hope that those who read and absorb this book would choose not to act withdrawn when approached by someone outside their circle of immediate interest. In the pages ahead I will share authentically dignified ways to end any conversation – however engaging or unpleasant – in effective yet elegant ways. There are tried-and-true approaches that won't compromise anyone's integrity or be likely to hurt another person's feelings. It is also my intention to talk about the scope of responsibility we have for the way a conversation goes, or a relationship develops... and, in the context of networking, to see rejection for what it is. It is the act of another person, *for which we should not bear any responsibility.* While rejection and other fears associated with networking will be addressed in detail later in the book, they're too important not to mention from the onset.

This is why it can feel so scary to network. Networking epitomizes our path through life in general: our fears of not being accepted; doubts about being 'enough'; anxiety about making it through the next challenge; dread of being rejected by others. The journey of getting good at networking – or adept at relationship building – can be like holding a mirror to yourself. We first learn things about ourselves, and then observe our interactions with others. Finally, we recognize which actions belong to us, which we are therefore accountable for, and which actions are outside the frame of this mirror's reflection, and thus outside the scope of our control.

Online and in-person networking scenarios can produce a high degree of anxiety precisely because we are faced with the perceived pressure of needing to be the best, most contained and most impressive version of ourselves.

Will I know what to say, or will my mouth dry out and my brain draw a blank, so I come across as a complete idiot?

Will I be able to string a sentence together without resorting to filler words, or without letting my accent/ manner of speaking/speech impairment do the talking? Will my cultural or socio-economic background define me before I stand a chance to define myself?

Will I be a bore? Will I be informative enough? Will I be able to hold someone's attention?

Will I find myself stuck with a bore, endlessly droning on about themselves, and not a bit interested in what I have to say?

Will I know how to leave the conversation politely and at the right time? Will I know how to take a budding professional relationship to the next level?

What will they all think of me?

Even a brief read-through of these questions spells out one simple truth: networking is not meant to be easy.

Just like any other craft that appears effortless when performed by a master, networking, as the art of building relationships, has layers upon layers of skills that, once practiced, become second nature. Until then, they are mere skills to be studied, learned and put to practice at every opportunity.

3

NETWORKING'S
BAD REP

I asked my friend John Nicolson, Scottish National Party Member of Parliament and Shadow Culture Secretary – who's also a journalist and former BBC and ITV news presenter – what networking meant to him. "I've always thought networking has rather negative connotations: pursuing relationships for personal advantage without necessarily having any interest in the person or people being targeted," he said. "I think of faux jollity, back slapping and an eye for the main chance."

John is very successful professionally, has a wide circle of friends and possesses that rare skill of putting every-one around him at ease. He is popular in any company, a wonderful conversationalist, and the epitome of a socially accomplished individual.

In my eyes, John is masterful at building relation-ships. He knows how to develop rapport with people, be authentically engaging and maintain connections through life's ups and downs.

Yet, for him and many others, the term 'networker' does not appear to reflect these skills. There is no doubt in my mind that the term 'networking' itself is a misno-mer. While a network is defined as "a usually informally interconnected group or association of persons (such as friends or professional colleagues),"[3] the act of network-ing assumes a completely different meaning.

The Merriam-Webster online dictionary defines it as "the exchange of information or services among individuals, groups, or institutions."[4] The Oxford English Dictionary describes networking as "the action or process of interacting with others to exchange information and develop professional or social contacts."[5]

Where did the jump from 'informally interconnected group' to 'interacting *with the purpose* of exchanging information and developing contacts' come from? The loaded action of *networking* seems a far cry from the original state of being in an interconnected group. And this is something many of us – even (especially!) those who thrive on authentic relationship building – have a problem with.

When I set off writing this book, I became a conduit for the irritation and bitterness people often felt about the topic of networking. I know exactly why those who spoke to me about this felt that way. The following passage, from a book called *The Power of Soft*, by lawyer and negotiation expert Hilary Gallo, explains it perfectly:

"As people become more objectified, our conversations become transactions about the thing we want to achieve rather than a human interaction within which a request is wrapped. The challenge is to keep asking ourselves what the people we are dealing with mean to us. If we get to a point where a person becomes either an obstacle, a vehicle or an irrelevance, then we are in danger of objectifying them. Treating people as mere objects is our modern disease. We rightly worry about the way women are objectified in the media but this is a very visible example of a much wider phenomenon. The more we act from the reason alone, wanting things from people, the stronger the urge is to treat them as a mere vehicle in that transaction."[6]

Networking is often seen as means to an end. At its crudest, it is viewed as the opportunity to make connections in order to reach a specific professional goal. There is occasionally a misplaced encouragement to see people as pieces in a complex board game, to enable 'the player' to get to the end faster and richer.

Truly successful networkers warn against this strategy. "Don't be too efficient," says research and consulting entrepreneur Keith Ferrazzi in his bestseller, *Never Eat Alone*. "Reaching out to others is not a numbers game. Your goal is to make genuine connections with people you can count on... If you're not making friends while connecting, best to resign yourself to dealing with people who don't care much about what happens to you. Being disliked will kill your connecting efforts before they begin. Alternatively, being liked can be the most potent, constructive force for getting business done."[7]

Throughout this book we will discuss our evolutionary predisposition to connect with the purpose of being a part of an interlinked society. There is the inherent pull of a deep, inner need to be part of 'our tribe,' because this is the source of safety, happiness, trust in the other and life satisfaction.

Curiously, trust in their networks helps people not only feel happier but also deal with such life-altering, all-consuming events as pandemics. According to *The Economist*, polls show that "many of the places that have coped best with COVID-19, such as Nordic countries and New Zealand, have widespread faith in institutions and strangers."[8]

To many, the whole notion of networking is self-serving and full of artifice. Yet, the meaning is ours for the choosing, and whilst we may not want to go as far as rewriting dictionaries, we can adopt a different lens.

In other words, we can begin seeing networking through the lens of a 21st century practitioner: as a path to connect with others. We can frame it as a set of people skills and a positive mindset to create, develop and sustain relationships that will enrich our lives, enrich other people's lives, and bring meaningful connection to our work or business. What's not to like?

4

MY STORY OF FAILURES (IT HAPPENS TO THE BEST OF US)

In 2000, I came to the UK to settle into a new life. Although I had spent a year in the late '90s studying at a university in the West Midlands, this was spent mostly in the company of fellow international students and, as such, I did not build a broader network of contacts. In fact, I only knew three people in the London area when I first stepped off the plane. I was anxious, I was lonely, but I was also excited. I had just graduated from a law school in Moscow, and couldn't wait to go out there and begin my career journey.

And so, I did. After more than 50 job applications and 20 or so interviews, having failed in the first, second and third rounds, I finally landed a job in the City. I was employed as an assistant in the fledging Russian department of a very traditional firm of legal professionals with some 200 years of history. The tradition-bound setup also meant that many of those who worked there either knew each other previously, had mutual friends or belonged to overlapping networks. By comparison, I was a complete outsider.

When I started attending networking events, I soon realized that my being an outsider extended far beyond the workplace. Coming from abroad, I didn't have an established circle of contacts from university days and could not leverage the connections of family and friends to meet the movers and shakers in my professional niche. It soon became clear that, in order to make any waves in the industry, I had to start building my own professional network from scratch.

My plan was to research where to go about doing so, and introduce myself to those who shared my professional goals and provided the right chance to meet like-minded connections and clients. It was a good, solid plan. However, like most plans, it needed many adjustments along the way.

I recall plucking up the courage to attend one of my first networking events at a chamber of commerce. It was a nerve-racking experience. After a few minutes spent desperately clutching my glass of bubbly, I finally caught the eye of the event's host. He graciously introduced himself, asked what I did for a living, and then offered to introduce me to a couple of people in the room. At the thought of needing to make small talk with strangers, my heart started beating faster, my mind went blank and I seemingly forgot my name, job title and the name of the company I worked for, all at once. In short, I was a complete wreck. I wanted to run for the nearest exit, but that wasn't an option.

What was the worst thing that could happen, I thought? Well, here are some of the scenarios I was fearing:

- My mouth dries up and I'm unable to string two words together

- I embarrass myself in front of these well-heeled potential clients

- I'm never able to show my face again at any of these events, forever remembered as the person who failed so miserably

In literature and films we're often led to believe that what we fear the most never happens. Instead, everything comes together at the last moment, and the underdog emerges as the winner, to everyone's delight.

In fact, here's the truth: in social situations, what we fear *is* likely to happen. In my experience, our outwards behaviour reflects our thinking. That is to say, if we think we will struggle to string two words together, we'll probably act out this expectation... just as I did at that ill-fated event. When the host introduced me to a potential client, I stumbled over my words, could not articulate what I did for a living and fumbled through my bag searching for a business card (to no avail). The brief chat finished with an awkward exchange of pleasantries and the promise to connect by email. Yet, as I walked away – feeling both relieved and mortified – I realized that I did not remember anything about that person; not his name, nor the company he was with. I felt like a complete and utter failure.

And what did that other person think? I will never know, but I can hazard a guess. He likely thought I was nervous, new to the networking scene and still learning the ropes of working the room with confidence.

And here's the crucial point: that abysmal experience in my first professional networking event did not shatter my career. I wasn't branded a disappointment or a complete failure. It did not destroy me. It did not even hold me back from becoming, with time, one of the most active members of that particular networking group.

I cannot help but notice that the paralyzing fear of being branded 'forever a failure,' which many of us feel in social situations, is virtually never reflected in reality. This is the case even if we don't nail it at first, falling short of the often unjustifiably high bar we set for ourselves. Our gawkiness and embarrassing behaviour are just momentary failures – idiosyncratic awkwardness and doing something not quite aligned with what's expected in a particular situation. These are all common, perfectly human occurrences. Yes, it is absolutely normal to occasionally find yourself feeling like a failure, being awkward or doing something embarrassing. And perhaps this 'occasional thing' does happen a little more often as you're making your way in the professional world, before you're fully immersed in it and have had the chance to learn its ways.

More to the point, what I am about to say next might go against everything you've ever heard about human interactions. We are led to believe that people make up their minds about us in the first few minutes (if not seconds) of meeting. It may be so on a subconscious level in routine communication, but in the professional world there are too many factors at play to afford the frivolity of making a snap decision and sticking to it.

The world of professional networking is the perfect ground to *develop* the impression that you leave on others, which will hopefully culminate in you coming across as someone who is enthusiastic, determined and seeking to make connections.

In my capacity as a mentor, I was recently asked by one of my protégés whether, in a networking situation, a perceived bad first impression will drive a nail in the coffin of future career success. Like so many young people, she was anxious about *getting it right* from the start. She admitted to fearing failure more than anything. Therefore, any situation where the possibility of this is hypothetically greater than the prospect of success immediately spells trouble. She was worried that she would rather avoid a positively life-changing encounter than risk social embarrassment.

This brought home uncomfortable memories from my own initial foray into the world of networking. The self-consciousness. The discomfort. That gnawing sense of uneasiness.

Like her, I'd put so much value on how I came across, thinking all would be lost based on an initial stumble. Turns out, I had many chances to develop my style and to nail the communication aspect of it all.

In my experience, even if an interaction does not go particularly well, people quickly move on. The vast majority of those you meet will quickly forget the detail of your first interaction. Moreover, the likelihood is that the next time you bump into them they will be delighted to see your familiar face. They would not have committed to memory the time you were lost for words or fumbled your elevator pitch, and will be glad to have an opportunity to get to know you better.

This is because, despite what we all think, we are not the main feature of anyone else's universe – only of our own. (Well, maybe also that of our parents' and our young children's worlds... but that's it!) It's worth remembering this next time we obsess over how we come across. The first impression blows over, and we are left with many more chances to practice the art of networking. The opportunity presents itself again and again, until we feel that we are showcasing our true self. And this is the ultimate goal.

WHAT 'GREAT' LOOKS LIKE: AUTHENTIC PEOPLE BUILD AUTHENTIC RELATIONSHIPS

I like to ask questions. This has been my superpower from very early on. True, when I was in primary school, overworked teachers sometimes rolled their eyes and sighed at my propensity to ask question after question, especially the kind others were too shy to bring up. By and large, that skill has served me well, and I am grateful for having this thirst to know the *hows* and the *whys*.

Writing this book has created rich opportunities to ask a lot of questions. I wanted to know whether what I knew empirically reflected other people's experiences. I strived to discover whether what I held true was widely-shared knowledge, or just my own biased, narrow opinion. I wanted to be as objective as possible for my readers, whilst still writing a treatise rooted in *my* 20 years of experience in professional services.

So, I decided to put my superpower to good use. I have long enjoyed observing how other people enter unfamiliar rooms, approach new people, exude friendliness and positivity, listen with compassion and appear to be in the permanent state of readiness to help with exactly the thing that's right at the moment, be it a useful introduction or sought-after advice. None of these people are 'networking professionals.' Their job does not consist of selling their product or service to a potential pool of customers, or orchestrating meet and greet events. They started off as regular professionals – lawyers, financiers, bankers, insurers, journalists, marketers, notaries and consultants – but went on to become tremendously successful and respected in their chosen field.

Through engaging in clever networking, some have become so popular in their industry that they've formed their own thriving networks, whilst others have massive followings both in real life and on social media. There is one thing that connects all of them: they have impressive professional standing. Much of their work comes from recommendations through their network of contacts, referrals by happy clients and being authorities in their respective fields.

The other common feature that links these people is the simple fact that one enjoys being around them. This is a quality that is hard to define, but to put it simply, they are *easy to like*. A big part of it is that they make others feel good in their company. These individuals are super successful, live rich and interesting lives, are brimming with fascinating ideas and have lofty ambitions. Yet, the irony is that, when you are in their company, *you* are the one who feels important, interesting, with a fascinating life story that is worthy of rapt attention.

In essence, this is what makes them likeable: they project interest in others, positivity and willingness to help, regardless of the immediate 'usefulness' of the other person.

That is why I call these people 'master networkers.'

But let's get one thing straight: none of these master networkers self-identify as such. They'll say they don't feel at all masterful at it, but most admit to thoroughly enjoying the act of building relationships. A close friend – a prominent corporate lawyer in the City – has said that, whilst he was not a fan of actual networking in the classic sense, he always had the relationship at the centre of his attention. "Understand what may be of interest to others," he suggests, "and ask yourself how you may fit in to bring value to them. In other words, why building a relationship with you may be of value to *them*."

This emphasis on the other person – making it first and foremost about them – is at the centre of being masterful. Whether you genuinely enjoy meeting other people or are more motivated by the adrenaline-pump of the chase, the emphasis must be on the other person. Only then will you click with contacts and allies who can be of genuine benefit to your business or career. Your interests are your business, but they do not feature in the process of building authentic relationships. The focus should always be on the interests and motivations of others.

One of my personal heroes, Dale Carnegie – author of the 1936 self-help classic *How to Win Friends and Influence People*, among the bestselling books of all time – identified one all-important law of human conduct. "If we obey that law, we shall almost never get into trouble," he said. "In fact, that law, if obeyed, will bring us countless friends and constant happiness. But the very instant we break the law, we shall get into endless trouble. The law is this: 'Always make the other person feel important.'"[9]

If there's one characteristic that stands out in people who are considered 'authentic,' it is their ability to be liked. This is a difficult concept to codify, as it is often hard to put into words what separates a person who is widely liked from one who doesn't elicit that response from others. "If only I knew the exact recipe for being liked," said one friend, "I would become the most successful person with my clients."

The truth is that there *is* a recipe. There are certain ingredients in a person's makeup that have been proven to make them likeable, influential and able to lead others. Let's go through the list together and see whether you can think of someone in your life who possesses that likeability factor:

- **AUTHENTICITY** ranks first on my list, and for a good reason. This is one hard-working word in a modern person's dictionary, but is it a surprise? An authentic person does not put on an act in an effort to be like someone else. Being authentic means knowing what is important to you, standing by your morals and expressing yourself without fear of being denounced for not adhering to an accepted, 'correct' point of view.

  Now, this can be a tall order in a society where *cancelling* is rife, and where thinking differently can subject one to vicious accusations and trolling. Social media is a powerful platform for spreading conventional opinions, effectively pushing anything else to the outer borders. Authenticity might be a fashionable term, but being true to yourself as an actual way of life can feel like going against the grain of what is considered fashionable... or even acceptable.

Thus, authenticity inevitably requires courage. To be yourself – to be authentic – is a brave path that is often challenged from both the outside and inside oneself.

The audacity to be yourself is not about sticking to your guns whatever the circumstances. It is about living with the acceptance that we humans are flawed by design. The complexity of us does not lend itself easily to perfection, so we're prone to saying wrong things at the most inopportune moments, stepping on other people's toes (literally and figuratively) and generally making mistakes. And this brings me to another point.

- **HUMILITY** is the single trait that can distinguish a mature individual from an immature one. Humility is something that some people find hard to arrive at, as it requires both self-awareness and the deep understanding of the effect that people have on each other. In a society where arrogance is prized and singing about individual achievement from the rooftops is the norm (where the likes of Instagram, Facebook and LinkedIn are seen as necessary paths to success, because what is success if nobody sees it, right?), demonstrating accountability and taking ownership of mistakes looks like going against the grain.

Yet, humility is the very essence of our connection to other humans. By demonstrating humility, we tell another person: "I am flawed, I'm imperfect, but I want to improve so that I can build a more genuine, more authentic relationship with you." Nothing is as powerful as admitting to another that the value of our relationship with them is our top priority.

- **HUMOUR.** It might surprise you, but this element is actually closely connected to humility. Not taking yourself too seriously, and being able to see humour even in challenging situations, shows true maturity of character.

Emily Torres, Managing Editor of the digital community *The Good Trade*, has this to say about the power of humour: "Taking yourself too seriously has little to do with how silly you actually are. You can be a wacky comic or a deadpan scholar and still take yourself too seriously (same goes for deadpan comics and wacky scholars). It's about the amount of control you try to take over things that are uncontrollable in your life – and how you respond to occurrences outside of your authority. If you freak out because someone suggests using a 'different cookie recipe than the one you know, just this once,' then you're probably taking yourself too seriously... Not taking yourself seriously doesn't mean you lack self-respect, or that you're ambivalent about who you are. It means that you see and accept yourself at your most elemental – as a changing human playing out an unfinished story."[10]

When you next spend time around those who normally draw people in, you won't be surprised to hear plenty of good-humoured jokes. Why does it matter so much? Because, deep down, we all know that we aren't perfect, and seeing another person being open, unguarded and light-hearted about this fact feels very comforting. And we all like emotional comfort.

• In my job, I come across a lot of famous people. I encounter actors, rock and pop stars, sporting heroes, supermodels, top fashion designers, TV stars, some of the richest people in the world, renowned businessmen and businesswomen, top politicians and royalty. The truth is, the laws of relationship-making apply to everyone. I've learned through experience that nothing is more attractive than someone who remains unpretentious and unaffected, regardless of their social status.

UNAFFECTEDNESS, or the lack of desperation to impress others and thus *be liked*, is a powerful statement that a person is comfortable in their skin. When this happens, others find it much easier to be comfortable around them, and therefore enjoy the experience. One of my favourite celebrity clients is a legendary fashion designer who, despite her status, is unpretentious enough to always find time to ask *me* questions about *myself*. Her ability to take the focus away from herself, not obsess about her 'persona,' and rather make it a part of her nature to pay attention to those around her, make her genuinely and positively unforgettable. The fact that her team has stayed with her for years, if not decades, speaks volumes about how much they enjoy working with her. In an industry where superficial and artificial can be the order of the day, standing out by being real and authentic is quite potent.

• Whilst some people have that difficult-to-put-your-finger-on quality of attracting and impressing others, **CHARISMA** is, in my opinion, developed over years, rather than something one is born with.

It encompasses general 'coolness,' or a degree of confidence that allows the person not to obsess about others. It requires courage in demonstrating emotionally laden leadership. Charismatic people are just as likely to elicit a strong negative response as positive reactions. They can be liked or disliked, but charisma plays a significant role in understanding likability.

When it comes to building professional relationships, possessing that likeability factor is like having a really strong foundation – it makes putting up walls, doors and building the roof so much easier! Yet, much as we cannot make a home from a foundation alone, being easily liked is not enough.

Research suggests that when we meet someone, our brain is wired to scan for signs of trustworthiness. This is an evolutionary response, over which we rarely have control. The upshot of this 'scanning' is to either establish that the person in front of us can be trusted or that he or she is not safe for us to engage with. Referring to safety here does not imply physical security, but rather psychological wellbeing. We feel psychologically safe when we're able to share our thoughts and ideas with someone, without the fear of being judged or having our ego bruised by lack of interest or attention. This is an interesting phenomenon. In the corporate jungle, we are just as attuned to the trustworthiness of others as our ancient ancestors would have been on the wild savannah, coming across an unknown individual from a different tribe.

In the context of professional networking, trustworthiness plays a twofold role.

First and foremost, a trustworthy person possesses integrity. This is someone who is able to keep promises, and be reliable, honest and principled, no matter how challenging the circumstances are. Integrity is also one of the most prominent elements of authenticity. You cannot be insincere and dishonest, or chose to be honest and sincere only when the circumstances are favourable, and expect to be seen as a genuine, authentic person. A lack of honesty, with yourself and others, is enough to be branded inauthentic.

The organizational consultant Keith Ferrazzi and journalist Tahl Raz examine this in one my favourite non-fiction books, *Never Eat Alone*. Ferrazzi is an impressive master networker in the classic sense: he has lived and breathed every word in his bestseller, and he writes from the heart. He speaks of candour, the quality of being open and frank, as the very definition of authenticity:

"Authenticity – the unvarnished presentation of truth – is not only scarce, it's supremely valuable. It's the alpha and the omega, the essence of leadership, sales, marketing – pretty much any discipline involved in motivating humans to do anything. Candour isn't just about saying what's true, but doing so as a matter of habit, in the risky, fluid moment that your opinion can have the most impact."[11]

It is not easy to show candour and be authentically honest as a matter of habit. I have observed people carving themselves a much easier path in life by being genuine only when it suited them. Their openness would ebb and flow, depending on how it played in particular circumstances, which meant that they would cleverly survive many a change of management. Still, they never gained the trust of their colleagues and clients, as anyone with a basic level of intuition could sense that what they were assuring someone of one day could change the next, if it no longer served their purposes. That habit of sticking to the party line, regardless of personal convictions, is one of the reasons many public officials are distrusted, and why likening someone to a politician is never a compliment.

It takes a strong mind and real commitment to be genuine, honest and authentic at all times. But in the final analysis, the effort is worth it.

Authentic people are like magnets. Others know they can be trusted, that they will feel safe in their company, that there will be no back-stabbing along the way. And who doesn't want to be associated with those they feel safe around? People seek out others who will not betray them; those who possess the moral fibre to be honest and truthful when it matters. This is no-brainer. If you want to create strong, authentic relationships, find the courage to be honest and principled.

Trustworthiness also plays a fundamental role in professional settings. When I announced to my clients that

I was leaving a firm where I'd worked for 20 years, I was astonished by many of the responses. I knew I had built robust relationships during my tenure there, and I was hoping I was not only liked on a personal level but trusted as a top professional in my field. However, we are British, after all, and effusive professional compliments simply aren't done! Nonetheless, the announcement of my departure prompted clients to verbalize their trust in my professionalism. In fact, many were open and frank in saying that they wanted to follow me to my new firm "because we trust you to be a top professional." That was a proud and humbling experience, and testament that developing trustworthy relationships with clients and colleagues quite literally pays.

Developing trust within your chosen field takes time and a committed mindset. However, this is a commitment that should be made at the start of one's journey through the professional world. Trust, like reputation, is hard to gain and easy to lose. Word of your trustworthiness will precede you. It will not only make the work of building authentic relationships much easier, it will also be a solid investment that will sustain you through different stages in your career... just as it has with me.

WE ARE MEANT TO CONNECT, NATURALLY

When I was a 20-something, I took huge pride in being self-reliant. When I immigrated to the UK at the tender age of 22, I only knew a handful of people. To begin with, I had no sponsors and no mentors, and building myself and my career up from scratch was something I aspired to and was thrilled with. Whether I was cognizant of this or not, enduring life's hardships as an independent 'unit of one' was a source of satisfaction and fulfilment. I had faith in getting things done by myself, and initially I found real joy in that self-confidence.

But as I started developing new relationships, I came to a fresh realization. I was beginning to embrace the joy of sharing. It was not only the good times that were worth celebrating in the company of those who cared about me, but also life's frustrations, the invading thoughts of self-doubt and philosophical perspectives on humanity and our role in it. By my late 20s, the tide started turning for me, and I was embracing the beauty of being a part of something bigger than myself. Surprisingly, my independence and self-reliance didn't suffer, and I was able to tap into these strengths whenever life demanded it. However, I no longer felt that my achievements were only worthy if I walked the path alone. Initially, it was only a vague inkling, but now I know with absolute certainty that the only achievements truly worth taking to the grave are the relationships we nurture from the heart.

I am not, of course, the first person to arrive at this wisdom. In 1938 – 84 years ago – scientists began tracking the health of 268 Harvard sophomores.[12] It was the tail end of the Great Depression, the worst economic downturn in the history of the industrialized world. People were disenchanted and exhausted, and to be a student during that tumultuous time – even in the ivory towers of Harvard – would have meant a heightened sense of uncertainty and anxiety about the future. Initially, the researchers were looking for clues to leading happy and healthy lives, but the study ended up going far beyond its original objective. It became one of the world's longest ongoing research projects of its sort, amassing a wealth of data on the keys to an adult's physical and mental health.

Robert Waldinger, the director of the study at the time, was a psychiatrist at Massachusetts General Hospital and Professor of Psychiatry at Harvard Medical School. Asked to summarize the findings, he concluded the following:

"The surprising finding is that our relationships and how happy we are in our relationships has a powerful influence on our health. Taking care of your body is important, but tending to your relationships is a form of self-care, too. That, I think, is the revelation."[13]

It confirmed something astoundingly simple, which many of us observe as we progress through life. We intuitively know that warm, functioning relationships with friends and family, more than anything else, keep us healthy and happy, so we have a natural propensity to seek out close attachments. No man is an island, no one is truly self-sufficient, and our reliance on each other is not only acceptable, it's essential for our wellbeing, both physically and mentally.

In the words of psychiatrist George Vaillant, who lead the Harvard study from 1972–2004, relationships play at least as important a role in healthy aging as factors like physical activity, avoidance of alcohol abuse and smoking, effective coping with life's stresses and maintaining a healthy weight. "When the study began, nobody cared about empathy or attachment," said Valliant. "But the key to healthy aging is relationships, relationships, relationships."[14]

As the full passage from 17th-century metaphysical poet John Donne's *Meditation 17* goes: "No man is an Island, entire of itself; every man is a piece of the continent, a part of the main." This old truism has stood the test of time, and is more relevant than ever. Isolationism does not lead to personal happiness, does not benefit the individual or the people around them, and can in fact have profoundly negative personal consequences.

We are meant to connect. Building relationships and building networks weaved of those relationships is what we are born to do.

In his life-affirming and brilliantly engrossing book, *Humankind: A Hopeful History*,[15] Dutch historian and writer Rutger Bregman cites a Siberian study of silver foxes that began in 1958 and continues to this day. Fierce predators in the wild, selective breeding by a team of biologists and geneticist demonstrated that the highest levels of friendliness in their background and upbringing yielded a cohort of foxes that were as friendly as puppies. Tail-wagging, affection-seeking, drooling fox cubs appeared as far removed from their vicious great-great grandparents as a domestic kitten is from a wild tiger. The incredible transformation, which became visible within four generations, astounded international scientists.

Geneticist Dmitry Belyaev cited the 'happy hormone' serotonin and the 'love hormone' oxytocin as suspected reasons for the astounding changes, and suggested that the same phenomenon could be observed in humans.

Supported by the most recent research, Bregman came up with a delightful term: 'Homo Puppy.' He said the feature that may have enabled Homo sapiens to outlive every other hominin species was... friendliness. Bregman argued that it wasn't the biggest brains or the most impressive brawn, as many would have guessed, but amiability, sociability and benevolence that helped make us the evolutionary survivors. Moreover, as with the silver foxes, scientists have discovered that the more *domesticated* humans became, the more our friendlier behaviour was reflected in certain physical and social changes, such as a longer period of reaching maturity, a more endearingly 'juvenile' facial appearance through life, and better communication.

"Human beings, it turns out, are ultrasocial learning machines," Bregman said. "We're born to learn, to bond and to play. Maybe it's not so strange, then, that blushing is the only human expression that's uniquely human. Blushing, after all, is quintessentially social – it's people showing they care what others think, which fosters trust and enables cooperation."[16]

It must be said that not everybody agrees with this position. When evolutionary biologist Richard Dawkins first published his highly influential book, *The Selfish Gene*, back in 1976, it was more Arctic blast than a warm hug for our species. It asserted that we were 'born selfish,' and this fact is merely the work of the genes. (It's the biology, stupid!) Dawkins discarded his theory of the innate human selfishness of humans in the subsequent editions of the book, but his original thesis remains a seminal piece of work. It sparked our fascination with what makes humans humane. Have we evolved, and do we thrive, through being kind and good to one another, or does the notion of *the survival of the fittest* still stand in the modern world?

Like every one of us, I've answered this question differently at different points of my life. In my early 20s, I was convinced that Darwin's theory of natural selection rocked. I learned early on, from the best: Maverick and Iceman, from the classic movie *Top Gun*, exchanging knowing glances when told on the first day of naval fighter pilots' school that "there are no points for second place."

Either/or was the binary motto to live by. It seemed natural that if you were not the winner then you were a loser and someone else should rightfully take your place. In the words of Tom Seaver, the legendary American baseball player, "There are only two places in the league – first place and no place."[17]

The more I journeyed through life, the more I realized that things were not entirely black-and-white; there were many colours on the spectrum of life's triumphs. Success that involves trampling anyone who gets in your way may seem like reaching the 'first place' that Seaver lionized, but this comes at a price. A life solely focussed on *win, win, win* at all costs, to the detriment of meaningful relationships with others, generates feelings of alienation, disconnection (see Chapter 8) and distrust. As a strong-willed and ambitious person, I certainly went through a stage where I believed I could have things my way, and my way only, if I tried hard enough.

In fact, I became so well equipped at getting what I wanted that I could have run a masterclass on the very in-vogue topic of assertiveness training!

The professional world of the noughties era, when I was climbing the career ladder, certainly appeared to encourage that kind of behaviour. I observed many egocentric and ruthless interactions, compassionless decision-making and a seemingly hardwired compulsion to push out those who dared to express a differing opinion. The premise of *thrive or die* was the driving force – the perceived key to professional success – and many aspiring young people found that they had no choice but to join the ranks of the cutthroat strivers.

This *Wolf of Wall Street* sort of aggressiveness ruled the City for quite some time. Thankfully, the last decade has seen things starting to improve. The #MeToo movement, scrutiny of the gender pay gap, diversity and inclusion training, and greater awareness of mental health issues have begun to force a reckoning with those who wield the power in powerful organizations. It is my heartfelt hope that in the years to come the professional world will progress much further. Having witnessed the ugliest side of an industry focussed on gaining power and enrichment to the detriment of being human, I couldn't be more excited about this long overdue change. It's about time we started investing in the one thing the experts tell us is absolutely essential for health and happiness: the relationships we build, nurture and enjoy.

YOUR SOCIAL CAPITAL

In the summer of 2021, some 18 months after the onset of the COVID-19 pandemic and following a seemingly successful vaccination campaign, hope started to build that there was light at the end of the tunnel. Conclusions about it all (now seen as woefully premature) were beginning to be drawn. In July, *The Economist* published an article headlined "Establishing the cause of death," which asked why some places suffered more from the virus than others. The answer, while complex, pointed to one simple factor: inequality. Economic inequality often impacts physical wellbeing, as well as an individual's position in the workplace. Predictably, lower socio-economic status amplified COVID's negative effects.

However, one element of inequality spotlighted in *The Economist*'s reporting was truly astonishing. It related to something we discussed earlier: the seemingly amorphous concept of social capital:

> "In areas of high inequality people are more likely to say they distrust strangers or to have little interest in civic engagement. Research published by IMF in 2016 suggests why: in places where people have very different lifestyles, they see little in common with each other. Weak social capital almost certainly reduces people's willingness to comply with viral control-measures, such as self-isolation or mask mandates, for which the private incentives to obey are weak."[18]

It seems that social capital is dramatically influencing how a society deals with one of the biggest catastrophes of modern times. If it is such a significant element in the welfare of entire societies, what effect can it have in *your* life?

Some years ago, I first heard a message that stopped me in my tracks: if you are looking for success, treat your social capital with as much foresight as your financial capital. Invest in it thoughtfully, cultivate it carefully, and enjoy the returns.

Most of us have heard the term social capital, and probably puzzled over what is means. Wikipedia presents pages upon pages of information on how it's been interpreted over the ages, and whether there is any merit in it. Turns out, there is even such thing as a dark side to social capital!

As the focus of this book is not theoretical concepts but the practice of developing essential life skills for professional success, we are taking a fresh look at the practical usage of well-known ideas and adapting them to the demands of the 21st century.

From that angle, your social capital comprises all of your connections; all the relationships you've been able to harness in order to lead a connected and socially fulfilled life. I am very careful here not to restrict these connections to their usage as weapons to deploy in promoting your career goals.

Your social capital is made up of your human-to-human relationships, which enrich your life on a daily basis and support you at different stages. They factor in joy, in success, when you're feeling down and need an emotional lift and, yes, when you need some help finding a new job or being introduced to a useful contact.

This is the point of well-developed social capital: you feel confident and secure enough about your connections that you can dip into that well any time you like.

Life is not a well-planned-out journey that goes off without a hitch. On your path to cultivating contacts and building relationships, you will surely have many bumpy rides. Some of those bumps will be so pronounced that they'll nearly throw you off the seat! However traumatic at the time, we should not be afraid of these experiences. We shouldn't be held back by the tangled, complex nature of even the simplest of human interactions. The real message is to see the value of the relationships we build and the relationships we have beyond the daily grind. The strength *is* in the complexity. That spells the truth of being human. This is the definition of authenticity.

For me, social capital comprises my relationships with everyone. Take my neighbours, for example. Sure, when we first moved in and wanted to get to know the people nearest to us, it was purely for the reason of establishing cordial neighbourly contact. With time, we found that one of our neighbours and I happened to have a mutual professional contact – the person I had been eyeing up as a potential professional mentor. Because we got on so well with the neighbour, I asked whether she could introduce me on a more personal level to this individual. Her response was a decisively positive one.

This is the value of our social capital in action: you feel strong, comfortable and secure enough in your relationships that you can reach out to your contacts for advice, a favour or help. You also feel strong, comfortable and secure enough to be ready to offer advice, give a favour or be open to help out when your contacts need it.

This beautifully simple, yet immensely powerful, way of life is what we call networking in the 21st century.

As simple as it may look, the social disconnect, anxiety and lack of role models when it comes to building and maintaining relationships leads to the current dilemma: we forgot how to lead life as socially connected individuals.

One of my inspirations in the professional world is Sue Langley OBE, Chairwoman of the insurance and consulting firm Gallagher UK and Alderwoman of Aldgate in the City of London. I first met Sue during her election campaign, and I was immediately struck by her disarmingly friendly manner. She is the rare example of someone with the charm to defuse the macho aggression that many City heavyweights are known for. Sue is humble yet immensely powerful, and I have seen her command everyone's attention in the room, despite being the most soft-spoken person there. Without betraying her authenticity, she has become a real force to be reckoned with in the overwhelmingly male-dominated world of the City, and beyond.

When I asked which of her personal qualities she credits with making the biggest difference in mastering network-ing, she put it very simply: "A genuine interest in people."

This is a powerful message for anyone seeking to build relationships with others and raise their social capital. Namely, redirecting your focus away from yourself and channelling curiosity into learning more about others is the single most effective skill you can develop. Sue says her motivation to network is that "I love meeting new people, I've learned so much [from this] and it's given me so many opportunities."

As with everything else in life, the decision to be pur-poseful about the social circle you build starts with the intention. All too often, this is the aspect of life that many of us simply don't give much thought to. We may fall into relationships with others out of convenience, or out of habit, when frequent daily contact turns into an established relationship. But, how many of us form relationships based on a true *interest* in others? Such outwards interest is always a reflection of our inner world – our aspirations, our ambitions, perhaps even our regrets and our desire to develop in a new direction.

Your journey to acquiring your social wealth starts with the simplest of tasks: being mindful of what interests you in other people.

What qualities in others do you find particularly attractive?

What characteristics do you want to emulate?

What questions do you want to ask a particular person?

But also, what puts you off? Which qualities in others do you particularly dislike?

The answers to these questions will give you more insight into yourself, your current values and your deepest concerns than almost anything else.

My intention is that this book will equip you with all the tools necessary to make you a savvy and genuine investor in your social capital. That social capital encompasses all links and connections with others, the values you share, and the understandings between you and others that enable you to trust each other. The notion that 'people do business with people' is an extremely important one – it perfectly captures why social capital matters in professional relationships. You do not have to be a starving-for-attention extrovert to appreciate the value behind this formula.

As with financial capital, the biggest value is derived from the wisest investments. That means that it's not the current bulk of your investments that matter most, but the returns they yield in the years to come.

Consider where you are on the risk spectrum, just as you would with financial investments. If you are a risk-loving daredevil, feel comfortable investing in emerging markets and are not put off by new financial products, go ahead! Fortune favours the brave.

To translate this model into the language of social capital, a risk-taker should be exploring a variety of networking platforms. These might include a gathering of players from tech start-ups you've never met before (but want to be a part of), or a conference that brings together an industry's bigwigs (if you want to get your foot in the door of that sector). If you identify as an extroverted individual, full of flair, then being energized through collaborating with others and having the ability to get people on your side quickly is your natural strength. Utilize it. Start building your social wealth by exploring the riskier, less travelled paths of access to various professional networks. It can feel scary at first, but the benefit of such an approach is that you'll boldly go where many others would not dare set foot. This will open the doors that other people are afraid to knock on – use this head-on approach to tackling social situations to your advantage.

But let's imagine that you prefer a more measured approach to risk-taking. If you're speaking to a financial advisor, you might opt for investments in more stable markets, through well-known funds, to extract the greatest value from industries with a proven track record. You might think of yourself as an ambivert –

one who has a balanced mix of extrovert and introvert in their personality. In this case, your 'social portfolio' would be full of established networks of people at your stage in their careers, and these would be safe yet exciting grounds to explore.

Finally, to the introverts among you... congratulations! You have superpowers that are often hidden, but that doesn't make these strengths any less potent. When it comes to building relationships, you prefer to go in slowly, and research thoroughly, before investing in what you believe to be safe and sound options. This can be a great strategy, often yielding fantastic results over time. Here, the secret is simply to *just do it*, and not to hold back because if feels too strange, too scary. Your comfort zone is precious, but it can hold you back from using your superpowers and making wonderful discoveries. Don't let the familiarity, safety and security of your comfort zone disadvantage you. Move at your own pace, but watch for opportunities and be proactive.

It's easy to feel overwhelmed with your networking goals, so this simple yet effective mindset of letting your appetite for risk guide you in building your capital wealth can help set a course that works best for you. This book is dedicated to authentic relationship-building, which would be an impossible task if you're blind to your own natural strengths. Harnessing the advantages of your true personality means that every relationship you build will have strong roots. And this is a recipe for becoming a successful 21st-century networker.

THE PROBLEM WITH DISCONNECTION AND SOCIAL ANXIETY:

HOW BEING COMPASSIONATE TO ONESELF CAN HELP

Whilst one pandemic might be on its way out sometime soon – or so we hope – I fear that another is only just beginning. This time around, the worst affected communities are some of the most developed in the world.

What is this pandemic, I hear you gasp? It is a malady that you already know well, as it has touched the lives of many. It is the scourge of disconnection.

The last 15 years has been the first time in the history of humanity when we have been genuinely connected to everyone and everything in the world, 24/7. Behold, the digital revolution! Living in Europe, we can reach out to friends and family in Australia within seconds, using the vast array of social platforms at our disposal.

With as many as 2.91 billion monthly users on Facebook alone,[19] the perception is that your 'friends' and contacts couldn't be easier to reach out to. As helpful as connecting on social media can be, as we've discovered over more than two years of pandemic-related lockdowns and travel restrictions, it can also mask a painful and ever-growing absence of authentic, real-life relationships.

Information overload and the carefully curated presence of your contacts on Facebook, Instagram and LinkedIn make it difficult to sort out what's real and what is not. More to the point, conducting most of our social life on a screen gives the *illusion* that we are relating and communicating. In reality, we're merely addressing a digital image, mostly devoid of all that makes human communication so unique. You can express compassion by typing 'sorry,' and attach a sad-face emoji, but you cannot give a comforting hug. You can share your innermost dreams by writing a list for someone to read, but they will never be able to see from a sparkle in your eyes how much it all matters to you. You can describe to another person your dream job, but they will never be able to truly relate to this if they don't hear your passion when you're talking about it.

There are jokes about the generation of digital natives struggling to express themselves without resorting to silly emojis, but is this so far-fetched?

As humans, we relate to one another on so many levels, and exactly *what* is being said is only a part of the message being delivered. The other elements of that message include the speaker's posture, tone of voice, hand gestures, eye contact and countless other signals that comprise interpersonal communication. True, we can communicate by staying silent, by words alone, by lowering our voice or by gazing sternly at someone, but each of these are individual piece-parts in the comprehensive toolbox of human engagement.

How ironic it is that through our over-exposure to social networks we are losing our ability to be social. This has been exacerbated by the pandemic – through over-reliance on technology we've quite literally forgotten how to really engage and communicate.

That is why, in this book on networking, we need to talk about the importance of talking to each other in person before we look at *how* to best do this.

Still, societal disconnection cannot be attributed solely to the disruption of the pandemic or the stratospheric rise in communication technology. Because knowledge is power, it is critical to understand not only the reasons why we are where we are as a society, but what we can do to affect immediate changes.

There is a compelling notion that one reason so many feel disconnected today is that "the common life that united our grandparents and their immediate ancestors is now withering away. We are less likely to join clubs and societies, and our schools and workplaces have become ever more divided by wealth and education."[20]

Those are the words of international consultant and governmental advisor Jon Yates, executive director of the UK's Youth Endowment Fund and co-founder of a series of charities designed to bring people together. He coined the term 'common life' to describe societal rituals, habits and institutions that counteract the 'People Like Me' (PLM) syndrome. This is the age-old concept of unconscious bias, where people who project the same appearance, thoughts and actions automatically like one another. Consciously or not, those who are alike in their beliefs, education levels, professional fields, political opinions, chosen lifestyles, likes and dislikes tend to 'flock together.'

Yates suggests that the disruptive changes society has been going through have had a cataclysmic effect on its wellbeing.

"When truly transformational change occurs – whether the move from foraging to farming (the Agrarian Revolution) or farming to factory work (the Industrial Revolution) — the common life that has so effectively brought us together simply doesn't fit anymore," Yates said. "It doesn't adapt and so it falls out of use. No new one springs up for many years. Societies face an interregnum – a transitional period with no common life. With no institutions to bring people together, society fractures. Violence and conflict spreads. We are today in an interregnum."[21]

But, as Albert Einstein wisely said, "In the midst of every crisis lies great opportunity." There is no doubt that when one feels fundamentally disconnected from society, situations that require interaction with others can cause tremendous anxiety. The natural response to this apprehension is to distance oneself from the perceived source. It's understandable, then, that many will resort to hiding behind a computer screen and a social network avatar as safe, comforting choices. In other words, we disengage because we feel safer when we are not connecting and interacting with others. This is especially true when we don't know the other parties well, and if they don't appear to share our lifestyle, education, professional aspirations or political views.

One of my personal heroes, the professor, lecturer, best-selling author and podcast host Brené Brown, put it this way in her 2012 book, *Daring Greatly*: "We disengage to protect ourselves from vulnerability, shame, and feeling lost and without purpose."[22]

For anyone looking to bridge the gap between disengagement and connecting, Brown said, the healing process begins by acknowledging that "we can't give people what we don't have. Who we are matters immeasurably more than what we know or who we want to be."[23]

Brown's central premise is that there's great power in showing 'weakness,' or what many of us perceive to be our weakness. She suggests that the ability to be authentic – showing the world who we really are – can be a transformative experience for the individual and society alike. Being brave enough to be vulnerable, to remove one's emotional armour, is one of the most daring challenges an adult can take on. Yet, it's entirely worth it, for the benefit of the person and for those around him or her. This is the starting point for anyone looking to build relationships: we need to begin by opening our hearts, and filling them with the courage to be ourselves, to be vulnerable and to be authentic. Only then can we set off on the journey to connect with others, reaping immeasurable benefits in the process.

Charles Darwin, the father of the science of evolution, is universally associated with the phrase "survival of the fittest." In fact, he never said it. He did, however, write that, "Those communities which included the greatest number of the most sympathetic members would flourish best and rear the greatest number of offspring."[24]

It's heartwarming and empowering to know that across the history of humanity, kindness, compassion, generosity and cooperation have played a greater role than selfishness and ruthlessness.

This knowledge is ours for the taking, and to make the most of. Jon Yates, who we discussed earlier, advocates building 'the strengthened society,' where at different ages people resolve to come together with those who share that stage of life with them, but do not necessarily come from the same social circle. This agreement to walk the path alongside someone hitherto unknown to you – and fundamentally different from you in many ways – is a powerful opportunity to connect with those we can learn from, or who can learn from us.

This is the very essence of networking: to take disconnected threads, the tangled pieces of a rope, and weave a web of relationships that enrich and improve on every level.

THE BIGGEST SECRET IS... KNOW YOUR PURPOSE

The more I became immersed in the process of writing this book, the more I became aware of the common values that were shared by those who have proven to be master networkers.

Back in the early 2000s, when the imperative to open up to networking became evident, I started looking for a strategy to get involved. I had to deal with the awful, debilitating nervousness that would overwhelm me every time I walked into a buzzing room full of people. It quickly became clear that going into panic mode every time I was faced with a prospect of talking to people simply wasn't an option. I needed a crutch, at least to start with. And help, as so often happens, arrived when I least expected it.

I sensed that my fear was rooted in excessive concern over how I was perceived by other people. In social situations, the moment I became the centre of attention – whether in one-to-one conversations or in group discussions – I was convinced that everyone was judging my accent, my dithering, my opinions, my gender, my age, my attire, what I was saying. In short, I was obsessed with how I *appeared* to others. Worst of all, I was convinced that I was being perceived as undeserving to be where I was, by virtue of being too junior, too female, too stupid, too foreign, too boring. The list went on and on. In the final analysis, I was suffering from a bad case of impostor syndrome – chronic feelings of self-doubt and incompetence that persist despite one's education, experience and accomplishments.

I recall a luncheon organized by a chamber of commerce that my firm was a member of, held at the UK Parliament's House of Lords (of all places). I was seated next to a very serious-looking man, whose badge stated that he was a CEO, or Chairman, or something equally important. I felt like I'd died a sudden death of shame by merely being *humble old me* in the company of such a distinguished person. Having stumbled through the obligatory round-the-table introductions, I stared intensely at the empty plate and the set of cutlery in front of me, wishing for the next two hours to fly by without anyone attempting to talk to me. No such luck – the big cheese next to me stuck his hand out in my direction and smiled a great big Hollywood smile. "Nice to meet you, Alisa!" he said, without so much as a glance at my badge. I had, of course, been too self-absorbed to remember anyone's name when they were introducing themselves around the table. "So, what made you to consider qualifying as a scrivener notary?" asked Mr Chairman.

I made some incoherent noises in response, praying that this was the end of our stilted conversation. It was, in fact, only the beginning... and the beginning of one of the most important lessons in my professional life.

Mr Chairman seemed to have had a genuine interest in the thinking behind my chosen career, and encouraged me to talk about my path into the profession and the reasons for being interested in that particular field. He shared his (impressive) professional history and then did something I found hugely surprising. He spoke candidly about his motivations for doing what he was doing, and alluded to some important personal circumstances that fired his interest in the profession. I found this fascinating, and entirely disarming. In the space of 15 minutes, I was immersed in the personal history of this initially intimidating stranger, and I was hooked.

"So, you didn't just fall into the world of banking, and then soldiered on and climbed up the ranks?" I blurted.

"Definitely not," he said, a savvy smile cutting across his face. "I was always playing my game. And what is your game, Alisa?"

"Umm... I've worked hard, I've now qualified in my profession, and in the future I want to do my job as well as I can," I replied earnestly.

"This is great. Nothing wrong with wanting to be the best you can be at your job. In fact, you must *always* be the best you can be at your job. But this is not enough. You must also have a game plan. Your *own* game plan, I should add. Because, Alisa, if you're not playing your own game, you will be playing someone else's."

In the years that have passed since that fateful lunch, I've come back to Mr Chairman's advice again and again. *Create your own game plan. Stick to it, and adjust it, if that's needed. But, above everything else, it must be the game that corresponds with your own values, goals and objectives. Otherwise, you will forever be a pawn in other people's game.*

That unexpected lesson has served me well. I took time to uncover what really motivated me, what my natural strengths were and where I could make a positive difference in the world. With these elements clarified, thought through and combined, I was then able to devise my *purpose* and attract the right opportunities. I was able to commit my time to the projects that promoted my purpose, developed me professionally and enhanced my worth – and, crucially, tapped into my values.

Today, in retrospect, I can say with utmost confidence that the best chances that my professional life presented me with were the ones that aligned with my purpose. To an outsider it might have looked like a sought-after promotion, an engaging project or a coveted volunteering role just fell into my lap. In fact, these all logically follow on when you start putting your decisions and actions through the test of fitting in with your purpose.

When you move through life as someone who knows their purpose, magic happens in your interactions with others, too. Because you're clearer on who you are, what matters to you, have a coherent plan of action and the direction of your travel through life is clear – you have a game plan – you naturally concentrate less on what others think of you. That nonsense simply doesn't matter as much, as you now have far more interesting and important things to concern yourself with!

"I have a million-dollar question!" I hear you shouting. And I suspected that you might.

So... how does one stumble across their purpose? It revolves around finding your core values.

In her book, *Leading the Workforce of the Future*, management and AI lecturer Brigette Tasha Hyacinth offers this simple but powerful guidance: "Fill in the blank. My life is ideal when I'm_____,"[25]

Career coach and senior *Forbes* contributor Kathy Caprino also has some great advice along those lines:

> "Your life purpose is one unifying theme or idea that exemplifies your key goals in life, a theme that has been evident almost from the beginning of your life. It's the specific way in which you engage with life that makes use of all that you are and draws on your unique experiences, talents, abilities and interests in a way that helps you achieve your highest goals while being of service of others."[26]

In this day and age, when we are sorely tempted to look to others for happiness, when our interest in how other people live often verges on obsession, nothing is as hard as distancing yourself from the opinions of others and daring to trust yourself above everyone else.

The one and only Tony Robbins calls this 'searching inwards.' The life coach and leadership consultant has said that "The questions 'What is my purpose in life?' and 'How can I be happy?' are actually the same – and they have the same answer. You can never truly understand how to find your purpose by listening to others' opinions and seeking outside approval. Everything you need is within yourself."[27]

Seeking and finding your purpose is a process that can take some time. How long, exactly, depends entirely on the individual, how ready and honest they are, their commitment and the incentive to push on through obstacles. And beware... there will be many obstacles. Hurdles might include the temptation to focus on: short-term goals or rewards; perceived lack of time or headspace to engage in the process; the push-and-pull of your own deep-seated needs; lack of ownership of your decisions; the encroaching 'scarcity' mindset; and an inability to let go of the things/people/activities that no longer serve your purpose.

Yet, the purpose-clarifying process is entirely worth it. But don't be fooled: it is *a process*, and I'll be the first to confess that mine is still very much a work in progress. And this is okay. We are not finished masterpieces. We're all growing, changing, adapting and, as we do so, our communication with others evolves and starts representing us – our true purpose – more and more accurately.

And this is exactly the point of finding our purpose – the more evident it is to us, the clearer we communicate with others. Knowing our purpose makes it easier to convey our message when we meet someone new, shifting the focus to the passion behind our purpose, rather than on what he or she might superficially think of us. It also allows us to formulate with more ease our professional game plan, to carry us in the right direction.

Research has shown that people with a clear sense of purpose, that in turn leads to formulation of specific goals and a structured plan to accomplish them, often earn up to ten times more than those who hadn't done that work.[28] In my view, this is a highly persuasive argument for making 'knowing your purpose' the main ingredient in your secret sauce for professional success.

10

BE A GIVER, BUT NOT A SELFLESS KIND

I first heard Richard Macklin, then a senior partner at a large City law firm and now the director and full-time leadership coach at FulfilledLeaders.com, when he was speaking at a business development conference for lawyers. He immediately spiked my attention with a series of truly life-changing insights.

It seemed like he was putting into clear, concise words the ambiguous concepts that had drifted through my subconsciousness. I was hooked. I later got in touch with Richard through LinkedIn, was candid about the impact his talk had on me, and asked for some coaching. At the time I was pondering a professional dilemma, and I felt he could help me work through it. I knew that Richard's time was precious, and I wasn't sure whether his sought-after sessions would be affordable for an individual, rather than corporate clients. Having carefully listened to why I was interested in his coaching, to my astonishment, he offered me a few coaching sessions for free. I was ecstatic, and my sessions with Richard became the catalyst for the biggest professional change in my 20-year career. I fully credit his insightful, intuitive expertise with helping me muster the confidence, decisiveness and strength to pursue a much-needed change.

We stayed in touch, and I later asked Richard about his philosophy when it comes to networking. Unsurprisingly, he is a believer in the notion of giving ahead of receiving. He put it this way: "It's about giving. Most people think that it's taking, but it is giving, and then, one day perhaps, receiving. Perhaps. But it's not taking.

And I think it's the one thing that many do not realize. It's something about putting your radar up and somehow it goes out onto the airwaves. I've always found this to be a supernatural force. Because you're doing this, your mind becomes open, so when something pops up, your mind is already open to receiving it."

Richard is a man who is walking his talk. By being generous with his time and his wisdom, he has given me the gift of awareness, which empowered me to take the next step in my career. In turn, by taking that next step, I have affected change that has had a positive impact on many other people, both inside and outside my profession. I've also been so impressed by his intuitive approach that I was delighted to recommend him to others who approached me with questions about leadership coaching. In this instance, the loop has closed effortlessly, showing up the magic of giving at its best.

When it comes to relationships, especially those in the professional world, giving your time, your expertise, access to your contacts and referrals to other professionals does not always yield immediate positive results. In fact, you rarely see the positive consequences of your altruistic behaviour in the short term. Nonetheless, as Richard put it, by adopting a giving attitude, you send out a signal that you're ready to consciously become a part of the interconnected world that we all already live in. In other words, although nothing actually changes from a physical perspective, and the link is rarely obvious, accepting that there is a counterbalance in life

– that there is receiving along with every giving – is a powerful action in itself.

I'd venture to say that most successful people would agree that helping others has advanced their success. How does the mechanism work, you ask? It all goes back to a focus on the greater good.

Patricia Lajara de Camilleri, Vice President of Human Resources at the fashion giant Ralph Lauren, shared this on LinkedIn: "Givers often achieve the top positions in society because they focus on the greater good. They cultivate and use their vast networks to benefit others as well as themselves. Success, therefore, is a far larger phenomenon than I had previously imagined. Rather than attaching a quantifiable measure, or status, to the notion of success, its reach is limitless and more powerful when shared amongst society."[29]

Ultimately, success is only a storyline. We all know that life is full of twists and turns, and no one is immune from a downhill phase. Those who give generously often have an army of grateful one-time strangers, who are only too pleased to extend a helping hand when the going gets tough for the giver.

This is because we naturally don't like to be 'in debt' when it comes to interactions, unless, of course, one is what's commonly known as *a taker*. Takers don't think twice about exploiting others to further their own interests. This can serve them well for some time, but soon enough their reputation catches up with them. Once you have lost your reputation in the professional world – or in any other setting, for that matter – it's all but impossible to regain it.

In my career, spanning more than 20 years in the professional services trenches, one thing has become obvious: you cannot hide your true intentions for long. When business life becomes intense, stressful situations demand intuitive decision-making. Those who arrive at key decisions through the prism of self-service will eventually come to be seen as untrustworthy, because nobody likes to be caught up in someone else's egocentric plan.

Organizational psychology professor Adam Grant, the author of *Give and Take: Why Helping Others Drives our Success*,[30] and his colleagues have shared on their website (Giveandtakeinc.com) their thoughts on avoiding 'giver burnout.' This is the state of apathy and resentment a selfless giver develops if he or she had not been taking enough care of themself.

If you aim for success as a life goal, rather than simply the temporary accumulation of certain benefits – for example, money, power or fame – it is essential that you take time to identify your natural tendencies. Do you have a propensity to take? Are you inclined to give only after you've received a benefit from the other person, using the quid pro quo ('this for that') principle? Or, do you often slide into all-out giving, self-sacrificing mode, forgetting your own needs along the way?

If you recognize yourself in any of the above, the good news is that there is a more effective option. You can in fact give of your time, advice, expertise and contacts in your network, and feel energized by your actions. Having a healthy relationship with the act of giving can produce bursts of serotonin and oxytocin, the feel-good/love hormones we discussed earlier. It is also a recipe for being a life-long giver, rather than expiring after a particular exhausting string of 'acts of kindness,' performed when you were already an empty vessel.

Notwithstanding the importance of giving as a committed networker, relationship builder and a connector, knowing your boundaries, your priorities and your capacity to give at a particular moment trumps everything.

Be a wise giver, know your limits, and act with that knowledge in mind. My personal rule of thumb is that if something can be done within five to ten minutes, I will do a favour for someone, regardless whether I know them well or not. This could be obtaining contact details, referring them to an appropriate expert, providing a brief opinion on my area of expertise, or even providing a positive, empowering comment on social media. I usually aim to complete two to three of these tasks while in a cab on my way to a meeting. I value my time and my priorities, and my strategy is to use a couple of 20-minute slots a week to address various questions that come to me.

There are weeks, however, when I am so thinly stretched that I have to be careful to use my energy to prioritize the most important areas of my life. I call this self-care, and I know that by being mindful of my needs – and self-protective of my time and my wellbeing at certain times – I am, in fact, extending my capacity in the long run. And that's to everyone's benefit.

The mindset of a self-aware giver is one of the most powerful tools on your journey to building and maintaining authentic, valuable relationships. Get the balance right and you will enrich your life, and the lives of many others, to no end. Get the balance wrong and you risk either burning out or developing a reputation as a solipsistic individual.

In a thought-piece titled "Givers Gain is Transformational," Dr Ivan Misner, the Founder of BNI, the world's leading business referral organization, said that the "simple, two-word phrase – Givers Gain® – was a game-changer in giving people a different framework relating to the way they network with others. Giving is an idea that proclaims we can be something bigger than ourselves. It's a reaffirmation that our lives have significant meaning and that, through the community, we can be our best selves. For people who get it, this philosophy unlocks a whole new world of meaning and opportunity."[31]

PART 2

THE HOWS OF WORKING ANY ROOM

11

A SHARED PLAYGROUND FOR EVERYONE

I have a professional friend who likes comparing a networking event with a children's playground. Like a playground, she says, everyone is there to 'play,' yet the specific objectives often vary from person to person. I think of watching my daughter dashing from the swings to the slide, then digging around in the sandpit, clearly trying to figure out how best to ask that confident-looking boy to borrow his bucket and spade.

This is a fun one, but also a very important image. One of the most commonly cited reasons for avoiding networking situations is the sentiment of feeling out of place. Now, how many children do you think feel out of place at a playground? How many of them think they 'don't belong there?' How many avoid running onto the slide because they don't know anyone else who is using it at the moment? How often do you hear a child refusing to dig around in the sand because they are not 'senior' (or 'junior,' as the case may be when it comes to a sandpit) enough? Sure, some shy children may feel more reluctant to explore everything straightaway, but the truth is that even the most reserved kid could be easily cajoled into giving the swings a go, especially if a trusted adult is nearby. To put it simply, you don't often see a child bashfully lingering on the edges of a fun-filled playground, staring into their beer (er... *ice cream*).

Why, then, do we behave so differently when faced with the prospect of networking?

In Part 1 of this book we looked at the *whys* of networking: why it may feel so scary, when it's such a natural thing for us to get involved in. In this next part we will look at the actual practice of networking – the *hows* of landing on your feet in a busy room full of unfamiliar faces, starting and holding a conversation, and dealing with unavoidable pitfalls every networker encounters.

One of my protégés once asked how I felt walking into a new room full of strangers. I suspect that, considering my experience in networking, she expected me to say something along the lines of, "I couldn't contain my excitement over finding new clients and establishing new friendships." And although excitement does come into it, it exists alongside all sorts of less-pleasant emotions. I still get nervous; I still sometimes wonder whether I've said 'the right thing.' I occasionally feel shy approaching an important person; it still hurts when someone is obviously not as eager to make my acquaintance as I am theirs. This is because I care about the outcome... and because, you know, *I'm only human*. In short, feeling all of these things is completely normal. It really is.

I love the term coined by Michael Gervais, a high-performance psychologist whose clients include world-record Olympians and Fortune 100 CEOs, to name but a few, for the anxiety that holds us back when we walk into that room full of strangers. It is *the fear of other people's opinions* (FOPO).[32] This term is quite handy, as it reflects that modern-day obsession with what other people think of you. As many of us can testify, not only does it affect how we perform during the fear-producing event itself, but it eventually leads us to lose our true self. By constantly looking to our left and our right, trying to interpret what other people are thinking about us, we are naturally dismissing the core of ourselves. Our talents, beliefs and values are being completely overlooked in favour of what the proverbial John or Jane are thinking.

In the next chapter we will look at how best to harness your talents and spin so-called 'personal weaknesses' on their head, in order to see them for what they are: unique personal strengths. Yet, there is an important point left to address here – how we view the room full of strangers.

Your mindset is everything. Many of us may have been conditioned to develop FOPO as a coping mechanism. And so, if we now step into a new room whilst consumed with the dreaded FOPO, we will give neither ourselves nor the other people a real chance. Potentially good relationships do not emerge out of fear. Fear does not produce fruitful connections and productive collaborations. It leads to distrust, and screams that you have something terrible to hide. Fear has no place in the open space where authentic relationships are born.

This is why seeing your networking space, be it a large conference hall or an intimate dinner party, as a *playground* where everyone is bound by the same goal

– to play! – is so critical. It's tempting to arrive at an event with the conviction that you are not worthy of a grownup conversation with all these important movers and shakers. Who among these VIPs could conceivably be interested in your humble opinion? It is so easy to downplay your importance and doubt your credibility. It's so easy to sabotage your chances of meeting someone interesting *and* useful by dismissing everyone in the room as superficial and shallow.

Instead, be like a child who is about to enter a playground. See all of the exciting, inviting things: the swings, the slide, the climbing frame, the ice-cream van, the sandpit. Note the presence of other equally excited and similarly apprehensive children, testing the equipment, giving things a go, managing to jump on the see-saw with someone of roughly the same weight and height, looking to have the most fun. Pay attention to how sliding down the tallest slide next to bigger kids really does not change the fun you're having. It probably enhances it! Check out those dangling from the climbing frame at different heights; this does not seem to hinder anyone's enjoyment of hanging out at their own chosen level.

The most significant thing of all is that everyone comes to the playground for the same reason. Everyone knows that there will be things to do, and there will be other children there. The swings will be free to use and everyone will have access to them. If someone had issues with the simple rules and opportunities of a playground, they would probably sit this experience out.

Now, go and apply the same thinking to the proverbial room full of strangers. If you are attending a networking event, everyone expects to be open to the idea of networking. Sure, there may be limited access to certain speakers or sponsors. Other than that, though, everyone expects to move about freely, speak to different people and generally mix it up. Naturally, everyone will be free to form opinions, but it's important to remember that networking events are there for a reason. Those who attend them expect to network. So, go and enjoy. And put your superpowers to best use while you do.

12

WHAT IF I AM AN INTROVERT?
(AND OTHER SUPERPOWERS)

As far as networking myths go, the one about it being the domain of extroverts amuses me the most. This is an apt platform to debunk this myth, alongside many others. Let's start with my favourite, about the extrovert, the introvert and... the ambivert!

Extroverts are the best at networking. This simply isn't true. To begin with, it is worth looking at exactly what it means to be an extrovert and introvert, as this is often misinterpreted. According to the Myers & Briggs Foundation, whose methodology helps people adapt their approach to different situations and audiences, extroverts are likely to feel that the following statement will define them:

"I like getting my energy from active involvement in events and having a lot of different activities. I'm excited when I'm around people and I like to energize other people. I like moving into action and making things happen. I generally feel at home in the world. I often understand a problem better when I can talk out loud about it and hear what others have to say."

Extroverts are by definition your classic outgoing personalities, lighting up the room, freely engaging with strangers and seemingly never growing tired of endless conversation. An extrovert will be heard doing most of the talking, flitting from person to person, bringing others together, keen to make introductions and telling everyone about their latest projects. An extrovert may be one of the last people to leave a networking event, seemingly never growing tired of the company of other people.

Introverts, on the other hand, would find it easy to relate to the following Myers & Briggs Foundation characterization:

"I like getting my energy from dealing with the ideas, pictures, memories and reactions that are inside my head, in my inner world. I often prefer doing things alone or with one or two people I feel comfortable with. I take time to reflect so that I have a clear idea of what I'll be doing when I decide to act. Ideas are almost solid things for me. Sometimes I like the idea of something better than the real thing."[33]

Although introversion should not be confused with shyness – reflection before action is an important concept to an introvert – these people are least likely to engage in multiple conversations back-to-back, and are often seen listening intently to the other person and spending more time in what looks like deep dialogue. The concept of small talk can be tortuous to a classic introvert, who might find it too shallow to serve a real purpose in getting to know someone.

It is interesting that not many of us identify as either purely extroverts or introverts. Research has shown that as many as two-thirds of the population are ambiverts, exhibiting qualities of both extroverts and introverts.[34] Ambiverts are flexibile in leaning towards their outgoing side or calling on their more reflective, reserved qualities, depending on the situation. In the context of networking, this can manifest in being engaging enough to express their ideas with energy and enthusiasm, and be the centre of attention in a group conversation, while also being able to flick on their listener's switch, to allow others to contribute.

Whilst all-out extroverts certainly do not make the best networkers, what does make the biggest difference is how self-aware the person is. I cannot stress this point enough. I like to call this ability to assess one's own strengths and limitations *the networker's superpower* (NS for short). Extroversion, introversion or ambiversion can be your networker's superpower; the only condition is that you need to be aware of it. Leverage the conventional notion of having a superpower... but if you don't know what your NS is, it cannot be your power, and it certainly cannot be *super*!

Self-awareness is key. If, after you've finished this chapter, you are still not sure of your type, I suggest taking some time to learn about these three psychological preferences (inwards, outwards, and a melding of both) and where you fall on the scale. Knowing exactly what your style of communication is will allow you to harness your strongest side when connecting with others. How does this work? Read on.

For example, let's say you determine that you are an extrovert. Great – you are well equipped to command the room. You enjoy the company of other people, embrace the small talk and a deep conversation with equal enthusiasm, can handle different topics and even multiple, overlapping conversations, and you have the energy to last for the duration of an event. These are all great positives. However, remember that every trait also has its share of negatives. Your downsides can include a lack of focus when listening to another person. Your attention can easily drift away from the topic, and you can come across as someone solely focussed on *me, me, me.* Yet, being aware of your natural shortcomings can help you address flaws in your communication style. You can train yourself to stay in the conversation, put special effort into being an active listener (more on this later), and make note to swiftly progress from the initial niceties to deeper conversations.

In short, your extroversion is your NS. Know it, harness and tame it, if necessary... but *use it.*

And what if you are an introvert? These individuals can grow to believe they aren't meant to be good networkers. Wrong... and I have an example that should quiet the most stubborn of doubters. One of the most impressive master networkers I know is Elizabeth Filippouli. She is a journalist, author and the founder and CEO of Global Thinkers Forum, a platform for current and future leaders to exchange ideas, promote excellence and provide women and youth with knowledge and access to networks. An acclaimed international speaker and a champion of women's empowerment through the Athena40 network, Elizabeth is warm, generous, charismatic and has an immensely likeable personality. I feel privileged to have developed a professional friendship with her.

When I asked Elizabeth about her earliest memories of relationship building in professional settings and her biggest challenge, she said the following: "Over the last 20 years I dedicated time and resources to build international networks through Global Thinkers Forum and Athena40. The reluctant networker, who started off as an introvert, grew into a dynamic connector and network creator. My main motive has been the joy to build bridges between people and open new opportunities for professionals from around the world – women and youth in particular. The 'flight or fight' syndrome is quite common. My advice is to always stay in the room and 'fight' against your fears and insecurities. Chill out, just be authentic, bring a genuine smile and make sure that you are a generous listener."

This is a masterclass in harnessing your NS – in this case, being an introvert. Introverts can be the most sublime networkers, as long as they have the required self-awareness to make the most of their strengths. Because they recharge and recover in solitude, before meeting new people they should take time alone to regain their energy. Remember to keep your energy up throughout the meeting, taking frequent breaks, if necessary, and refuelling on snacks and water. And then, take a moment to plan your post-event recovery.

As you are unlikely to be naturally inclined to bounce from conversation to conversation, like an extroverted social butterfly, go into the event with reasonable expectations. It is better to have two to three good conversations, and feel connections being made that can be developed further, than have the goal of collecting 20 business cards. Remember that your NS comes with certain conditions of use, so prepare to make the most of your superpower by doing your homework prior to the event. Check out the profiles of attendees, think of those that interest you the most, prepare icebreakers and have some unusual questions that will make your interactions more effective and memorable. Finally, keep in mind that networking is all about building relationships, rather than shallow chitchat, and this is your strength. Use your NS of listening intently, asking pertinent questions and developing the conversation based on what the other person says, in order to build a strong connection. This connection will be what leads to a mutually fulfilling and beneficial relationship in the future.

And what if you are an ambivert? You lucky soul! Ambiverts have been proven to be the most successful as salespeople,[35] and it's easy to see how the blended characteristics of an extrovert and an introvert would be advantageous. True, the degree of ambiversion differs from person to person, so this makes for an even more compelling case to know yourself well. This knowledge cannot be theoretical, though, and it will develop the more you engage in networking. The real challenge for an ambivert is to harness the varying degrees of introversion and extroversion and make the most appropriate use of them in each particular situation. Self-awareness is key – the more attention you pay to your natural inclinations, the more you'll be able to direct your energy into a compelling presence and effective communication style. Be dazzling and enthusiastic when this is called for, and attentive and intuitive when that's more appropriate.

Yet, your psychological preferences are only some of the elements of your personal superpower. The other aspects could be viewed under the umbrella term 'otherness.' Being a woman in a men's world; being gay in traditionally heterosexual settings; being a person of colour in a sea of white faces; having a foreign or regional accent among the plummy, cut-glass voices. These are all personal characteristics that others may use to discriminate against you... or you can turn them into your Networker's Superpower.

At the end of the day, networking is about connecting with other people, not stockpiling business cards. Some decades ago, an extroverted white heterosexual male with a posh accent probably stood the best chance of being accepted in a room full of other extroverted white heterosexual men with posh accents. Thankfully, these times are (almost!) long gone.

Today's proverbial rooms, be they real or virtual, are full of people from different walks of life wanting to connect with other people from different walks of life. Your background and your purpose are what distinguish you from everyone else. So, by all means use these wisely. Instead of holding you back, your otherness can be your NS.

Craft your purpose. Know what distinguishes you from others. Strike a balance between your introverted and extroverted sides. Think things through, centre yourself and summon your inner confidence. Mix thoroughly, and turn this into your Networker's Superpower.

THE MOST IMPORTANT RULES OF NETWORKING:

HOW TO READ THE ROOM AND SPEAK TO ANYONE WITH EASE AND GRACE

When I talk to others about networking, the matter of starting a conversation inevitably takes centre stage. Face it: talking to strangers is not easy. That's the case for a variety of reasons:

- Most of us are brought up to be reasonably wary of those we don't know

- We can be hesitant to start a conversation

- You might be unsure of how to bring up relevant topics without appearing pushy

- Many struggle with steering a conversation to find out more about overlapping professional interests

- There is the classic fear of being unwanted and rejected

- And – how dreadful – what if we get stuck with the most boring person in the room for the rest of the night?

And the list goes on. We have all felt the weight of these 'what if' questions at some point. To have this niggling voice in your head is to be human. But if you let that voice guide your actions, you risk falling into the trap of self-sabotaging defeatism.

As my colleague Sina once said, it all starts with the right mindset. I agree wholeheartedly. As with everything else in life, a lot of things *could* go wrong when it comes to networking. You could spill your drink, lose your voice, get stuck in an uncomfortable silence for what feels like an eternity, have nothing to say, forget the other person's name, forget *your own* name, and generally feel lost in the sea of unfamiliar faces.

What if I told you that *all of these* have happened to me? (Well, apart from forgetting my own name.) What if I admitted that I have been where you fear you might end up, and then some? But here I am, *writing a book on networking*, having survived and thrived, and lived to tell the story.

It's tempting to let these fears lead the way, but I'm living proof that even the most embarrassing of situations will not kill your reputation as an aspiring networker. When it comes to social situations, having lived through the ordeal of doing things wrong enriches your experience. It changes your mindset to one of more compassion for others and, remarkable as it sounds, it's likely to make you a *better networker*. Navigating the awkwardness and the fear equips you with first-hand knowledge of how we, as humans, work. Having lived through the experience of forgetting the name of the person you've been speaking to for the last 20 minutes – and getting caught red-handed, when you're suddenly asked to introduce them – you will be more forgiving when someone forgets yours.

But, you will also be more mindful of remembering names when people are introduced to you. And Dale Carnegie's principle, "Remember that a person's name is to that person the sweetest and most important sound in any language,"[36] will become a powerful piece of social knowledge.

There are indeed many ways to 'fail' when entering the room, but very few of these are socially fatal. Most social embarrassments are survivable, and in fact quickly forgotten by others.

Yet, the purpose of this book is to make your experience with networking and building relationships not only effective, but also pleasant – joyful, even. As we have learned, making connections is the most natural thing we're born to do, and regardless of how inexperienced or rusty we may be, it's a skill well worth nurturing.

When you are faced with walking into a new room, it pays to follow a tried-and-true set of rules.

I have heard in the past that *there are no rules* when it comes to networking; that everyone should assume their own style and do what feels natural. For many of us, though, networking situations are not 'natural,' insofar as they're not a part of our daily routine. So, aiming to do what comes naturally for many might involve hiding in the furthest corner of the room, clutching a glass of something that helps with the nerves, and timidly observing everyone from a safe distance.

I want to say the following, loud and clear: if you're reading this book, you can do *a lot better* than that.

There are, of course, rules that govern effectively entering a room, reading the room and starting a conversation with just about anyone. You don't need an advanced degree to understand them; there's no lofty treatise on mastering the most important ones. They are rooted in common sense, they're easy to remember, and once you start practising, you will see the results from day one.

In fact, knowing the rules and practising them will help make networking your second nature.

There are three such rules that I want to share with you in this chapter.

RULE 1:
READY UP

It's human nature to feel safest when we plan for things to go wrong.

"Hope for the best, but prepare for the worst," as the old proverb goes. For many, that preparation involves a deep dive — imagining *all the things* that could conceivably go wrong.

Indeed, why oh why do we never prepare to be easily liked, meet fascinating people, have interesting conversations and plant seeds for great relationships, when we can indulge in anticipating a dry throat, a pounding heart and a memory like a leaky sieve?

Put it that way, it's easy to see how unproductive it is to let your mind to drift into dank, dark alleys of doom and gloom. You need to be proactive, and start readying up for a big event by imagining that things *go right*!

Whether or not you are excited about an event, everyone will benefit from taking some time to imagine walking into the room confidently, introducing yourself with the conviction that you deserve to be there, and having an open mind about connecting with interesting people.

Mental readiness is a huge step towards developing the confidence to form relationships with others. To start with, merely being aware of counterproductive thinking will be helpful. As time passes, build from the awareness of what you are saying to yourself before the event, to actively getting into a positive mindset. Actually *looking forwards to* meeting others will help you develop a genuine smile and a sparkle in your eyes, literally transforming yourself into someone people want to talk to.

Being ready also means having a tight, punchy elevator pitch up your sleeve. This is your personal statement of self-identification; your verbal business card. As the name suggests, it should last as long as a short ride in a lift - ideally, 20-30 seconds. Granted, this isn't long, so your focus will be on crafting something that is truthful, unique to you, compelling and memorable.

Having done the necessary work on your purpose, creating your elevator pitch should be a natural extension of that. However, the first step is to introduce yourself. This is a factual statement: a sentence about who you are and what your professional role is. Next, if you're representing a company, mention that. If it's not a household name, be prepared to succinctly tell what it does, in a half-dozen or so words.

Finally, state what distinguishes your company from others in that field. This naturally leads to how you and your firm can bring value to the other person, which is bound to pique their interest. But don't abandon your pitch there. Finish off with an exciting fact about your business, and a personal mission statement. This is where your purpose really comes in – the chance to seal your elevator pitch with a sentence about what really matters to you.

As an example, this is my current elevator pitch:

"I'm Alisa Grafton. I'm a Partner and Head of the Russia/CIS Practice at De Pinna Notaries, a 250-year-old London firm that has the biggest team of Scrivener Notaries. We take a modern approach to business, and have more than 3,000 international business clients, including companies in the FTSE 100 and many high-net-worth individuals. We're the only notary firm in London accredited with the industry's top information security management standard in all areas of our business. On a personal level, I enjoy networking, and I'm the author of a recent book on networking for 21st century."

Once you have your pitch ready, feel free to refine and rework is as you use it in public, and find the right version that works the best for you.

RULE 2:
READ THE ROOM

When walking into a room, one of the best things you can do is *have focus*. This means knowing who you would like to meet, and why. As mentioned earlier, the easiest way to do this is to go through the attendee list beforehand and make note of who stands out. Remember, this should be a wish list to keep your attention focussed, not a set-in-stone to-do list.

Alternately, you can always approach the event's organizers and ask them to introduce you to someone. They are there to assist with just that sort of thing, and are normally delighted to help.

If you came with a friend, remember not to huddle together and waste this valuable chance to meet others. By all means, feel free to speak to each other at the start of the event, and touch base to support each other at different stages, but resist the temptation to avoid others because you already have someone to talk to.

I know well that speaking to strangers can be an unsettling experience. But remember, *it takes two to tango*. A simple truth about starting a conversation that leads to a connection, that then leads to forming a great relationship, is this: the other person needs to be ready to talk. As you enter the room – a physical room, in this case – observation is key.

Have you ever been so engaged in a conversation that when it's interrupted it feels like an intrusion? In a social context, it is expected that the new person who joined will be paid attention to and involved in a conversation. However, when someone crashes the party in this way, it can be hard for those involved in the initial conversation to make that switch immediately.

As a rule of thumb, *reading the room* is the first thing that you need to do, before approaching a group of people to introduce yourself. How do you read the room? Think about grabbing a drink as you enter and positioning yourself where you have a view of the entire scene. Then, take a few moments to watch the dynamic. Who stands by themselves, looking like they would appreciate being spoken to by a braver soul? Who is engaged in a private conversation, where two or more people face each other squarely, their attention sharply focussed within this circle? Which pair or group of people has an open side, with people looking out from the huddle, ready to welcome new joiners?

It goes without saying that it's much easier to approach a person who stands by him/herself, or a group that is not intensely concentrating on a conversation.

Granted, this will be a tricky thing to sort out if you are just learning the ropes of reading the room. And so, it really is okay to ask. Posing a question along the lines of, "Can I join you?" is all that it usually takes. The answer will generally be, "Of course." If the response is more ambivalent, this is an opportunity for you to exercise your skill at reading between the lines. Remembering that it takes two to tango, and that you're unlikely to have an interesting conversation with someone who is not 100% invested in it, you can always suggest that you'll come back to that group in a bit, when their conversation is finished. If I feel that I am stepping on someone's toes by joining their group at that particular moment, I might say that I'm going to grab a drink, or just spotted a friend and need to say hi, and I'll be back in a minute. This leaves you with the option to rejoin this group, if and when it appears more open to a new person.

In networking situations, it's okay to 'form an orderly queue' to speak to someone popular. It's perfectly acceptable – in fact, often expected – that one might hover nearby and wait their turn. In fact, I have found it to be an effective way to catch a busy networker's eye if I want to talk to him or her. It will help that person subtly manage other conversations, and turn to you when appropriate.

RULE 3:
AIM FOR A LIGHT BUT INTERESTING CONVERSATION

Conversation is key to connecting with others. I can almost see your rolled eyes at how obvious that seems. However, obvious is not the same as 'simple.' So, in the next few chapters I will take you step-by-step through learning how to speak to anyone with ease and grace.

We will dissect the magic of small talk, examine the skill of transitioning into deeper, interesting conversation, focus on attention-giving as the prerequisite for... well, just about everything. And, we'll look at eventually mastering the art of becoming positively memorable. I'm excited just writing about these skills, as developing them will have an astonishing effect on your ability to nurture relationships within your chosen network.

SMALL TALK VERSUS MEANINGFUL CONVERSATIONS

I used to be very confused about the concept of small talk. Viewed from the Russian cultural prospective of my earlier life, small talk appeared indulgent, unnecessary and downright selfish. How can you waste someone's precious time droning on about the weather, I wondered. Wasn't it obvious that the best way to show a busy person respect is by going straight to business, and staying there?

I must say, in the last couple of decades my views on this have changed dramatically. Small talk plays such a crucial role in connecting people that it should really get an award for Best Supporting Actor.

It's true! Behind every Oscar for Main Conversation About The Important Things there is a humble trophy for Best Supporting Small Talk.

In its acceptance speech, small talk would describe itself as 'a phatic communication'[37] – a routine politeness – and explain that it merely serves a social function as a benign pleasantry. It would explain that it does not seek or offer information of significant value. Rather, its primary role is to serve as a bonding ritual and a tool to find out more about the other person.

Despite its humble self-definition, small talk is a powerful actor. It is the secret used by the best communicators to put others at ease, and to find out as much as possible about the person in front of them, all while keeping things light and superficial. Does the person have introverted or extroverted characteristics? Are they a 'thinker' or a 'feeler?' Are they most comfortable talking or listening? There are zillions of bits of information that you can draw from a brief but skilfully conducted interlude of small talk. Good small talk can really pave the way for an engaging, interesting and productive conversation – one that has every chance of flourishing into a great relationship.

Here are a few things to bear in mind when building your small talk skills:

- Positivity is key. Our mood is contagious, and if we approach any interaction dreading how awkward it's going to be, it's likely to become awkward indeed. Wearing a mask of trepidation is likely rub off on others, and shape how relaxed or nervous they are in your company.

  Instead, *fake it till you make it*! Smile, smile, smile. Smiling attracts good, interesting people like a magnet, because, both consciously and subconsciously, good, positive people like to spend time with other positive people. Smiling is absolutely the best head start you could give your fledging conversation.

- Speaking of good people, why do we often imagine strangers to be full of dark secrets and weird ways? A stranger is merely a person you haven't yet gotten to know. Assume that the person you're talking to is one of the good ones; expect the best in him or her. If they come up with an awkward remark, or maintain uncomfortable silence when you aren't speaking, resists the temptation to hook a label on that person. Cut them some slack. The first time you talk to somebody, a light, convivial mood is really all you're aiming for.

- When do we feel most relaxed and joyful? Yes, it's when we are talking to a good old friend about nice things we have in common. So, this is the mood to channel – as quickly as possible, try to establish things that connect the two of you. Do you both come from the same town or region? Do they also have a dog? Did they think that the digital marketing session was the best part of the conference so far? The point is to look for common ground and just enjoy exploring it.

- My favourite personal shortcut to feeling instantly connected to a person is to give them a genuine compliment. Be it a kind word about the colour of their jacket or the presentation they've just given, everyone enjoys being appreciated. At the same time, you convey that you share similar tastes or points of view, and this is precisely the common ground we're talking about.

- Small talk does not have to be about the weather or how bad the traffic was on the way to the event. Aim to stay current, and feel free to express an educated opinion about a non-inflammatory topic. Depending on the audience, it could be the theme of the event, the city where you find yourself, art or music – anything light, non-divisive and engaging.

- Small talk presents a great opportunity to interject some humour into things and show your personality. Georgie Nightingall, who is designing and running a course on small talk for BPP University Law School, says it's important to be "willing to offer something about who you really are."[38] She suggests answering the "How are you?" question with a number between one and ten, as an opportunity for a bigger conversation on how one measures the quality of a day.

- And, here's a closely guarded secret of many experienced networkers: once you have expressed your light, educated opinion, *listen* to the other person. Be interested – immersed, even – in whatever they are saying. Ultimately, we're the centre of our own universes, and it feels really good to see someone else thinking the same as we do about something. People often forget precisely what you say, but they will remember how you made them feel.

- Small talk, as with everything else, only gets better with practice. So, commit to engaging in the ritual as frequently as possible. You might feel awkward at first, but you'll slowly become more confident, until one day you'll actually look forwards to striking a light conversation with a complete stranger who one day might become your friend.

To conclude, small talk is big. If you put time into practising the ideas in this book at every opportunity, your small talk will develop into an effective skill. It will become the springboard that will allow you to dive into a huge pool of potentially valuable relationships.

But, small talk is not an aim in itself. It's a launch pad for a bigger conversation that will have resonance, meaning, and the significance to lead to a true connection.

I have often found small talk essential in providing me with as much information as possible about the person that I am speaking to:

- Do they seem keen to talk more than listen? Ask them a question that is focussed on them.

- Do they come across as a little reserved? Feel free to express a considered opinion about an easy subject, using gentle humour to melt the ice.

- Do they use the verb 'feel' more often that 'think?' This means they're likely more comfortable answering a question along the lines of, "Do you feel that this event has represented the industry well?" rather than "Do you *think* that..."

- Do they mention their profession, job title, place of birth or residence, a family member or a pet soon into the exchange of small talk? This signals what they're interested in and comfortable talking about, so steer the discussion in that direction.

By listening carefully to what someone's saying during the initial small talk, you can get a pretty accurate idea of what matters the most to them. This information is like a hidden treasure to anyone who is ambitious about building authentic relationships. As we have discovered in the previous chapters, such relationships are built around the things that are genuinely important to people. Therefore, as soon as you get a sense of what's most important to the person in front of you, as well as *how* they prefer to communicate, you have acquired the code to open the lock. What you do with this information next is another important consideration.

I am amazed how often conversations are abandoned at the small-talk stage! Just as we start getting a feel for how someone operates, many people decide to take off and find someone else to talk to. I have certainly done this once or twice in my life as a networker. And so, I know from experience that the missed opportunity to unlock the relationship whilst you hold the key is a recipe for ineffective networking.

The truth is that relationships are not built on small talk. It's a great door opener, but a relationship is built on meaningful conversations.

A 2021 research paper titled 'Overly Shallow? Miscalibrated Expectations Create a Barrier to Deeper Conversation,' published in *The Journal of Personality and Social Psychology*,[39] argues that because people are wired to be social and to reciprocate, sharing something meaningful and personally important in a conversation is likely to lead to the other person responding in kind. The majority of those participating in the study felt that talking about profound subjects created the right foundation for a stronger sense of connection.

The paper noted that strangers talking for the first time "reported feeling more positive, less awkward, and more connected to each other after a relatively deep conversation than they expected, especially when they were communicating over a relatively more intimate (voice-based) communication media compared with less intimate (text-based) media."[40]

Perhaps unsurprisingly, many participants were initially concerned that opening up to their interviewer and talking about more intimate topics would lead to a feeling of awkwardness, which would get in the way of the initial interpersonal connection. However, the exact opposite was the case. They generally underestimated the positive experiences of connectedness and happiness that engaging in deeper conversations brings, and often woefully overestimated the degree of awkwardness felt during profound conversations, compared to small talk.

"We document that people undervalue the positive consequences of conversations, especially deep conversations," the researchers concluded, "at least partly because they underestimate how much strangers in conversation will be interested in the content of the conversation, and care about the intimate information being shared. We believe this is part of a broader tendency to underestimate others' sociality, thereby creating a wide variety of psychological barriers to social engagement... [P]eople underestimate how positive others will feel following an expression of gratitude, a random act of kindness, a compliment, a trusting disclosure of a negative secret, and even a constructive confrontation in an established relationship... People expect others to be more indifferent to these pro-social acts than others actually are, just as we found for deep conversation."[41]

My experience matches these findings. Whilst you are setting the scene with small talk, the profound conversation is what takes things to a new level – the turning point where this relationship is likely to become meaningful and productive. But how do we make that leap without appearing too prescriptive in teasing out more personal information?

It is easier than you think. Think of the 'wh' questions as your rule of thumb:

- **Wh**en did you realize you wanted to become...?

- **Wh**o has been your biggest inspiration?

- **Wh**y are you focussing on developing...?

- **Wh**at are the biggest challenges for your business now? (Or, **Wh**at has been going really well for your company?)

- **Wh**ere do you see your company being in five years' time?

The primary purpose behind these questions is to learn more about the person in front of you. As we have discovered, networking is another word for relationship building, but how do you establish a real relationship with someone when you only know that he works in sales and hates rainy days?

Delving into meatier subjects, asking more profound questions and being interested in the personal journey of a stranger are highly effective tools. The 'wh' questions are by no means the limit, but they are a good starting point. They're easy to remember, often flow on from each other, and indicate genuine interest in wanting to learn more. The idea is not to get a sense whether a person is or might one day become 'useful,' but rather *to connect.* Connection means building on the basics you've uncovered during the small-talk exchange (think of this as crack-opening a door), and to be more purposeful about discovering where the personal and professional interests lie (akin to pushing a door open a bit more).

The degree to which you might be feeling confident and comfortable pushing that door open will depend on both your personal tolerance for deeper conversations and the other's readiness to talk. One thing is certain: sincerity cannot be faked. Learning to ask questions that show your genuine interest in someone is a journey of trial and error, but it's one worth travelling, for the destination is the ability to turn strangers into people with whom you have a connection in the space of 20 minutes.

The 'Miscalibrated Expectations' report referenced above went on to say this: "If you think that a deep conversation is likely to be especially awkward, then you are unlikely to give yourself the chance to find out that you might be a little bit wrong. Only by engaging with others do people accurately understand the consequences of doing so. Second, strengthening social relationships is critical for wellbeing, meaning that a reluctance to engage more deeply with others may leave people being less social than would be optimal for their own wellbeing. Being willing to dig a little deeper than one might normally go in conversation brings the opportunity to create a stronger sense of connection with others, especially with strangers."[42]

Whilst asking good questions is an especially effective tool in connecting to a stranger, *genuine interest* is the key. We all like to be understood, and this wisdom has been my guiding principal for as long as I remember myself as a networker.

The next chapter is dedicated to paying (and expecting!) genuine attention on the path to connecting with another person. Like most of the things discussed in this book, this may seem to be a no-brainer, but it can be remarkably difficult to put into practice.

CURIOUSER AND CURIOUSER

If there is one useful takeaway in everything we're covering, let it be this: networking really is shorthand for 'relationship building.'

The rules of networking include understanding the value of relationships in our lives, the skills of connecting with others and developing new relationships, as well as maintaining existing ones and being able to both ask for help and offer it. These are fundamental, simple knacks that become art when sufficiently practiced.

They rise to the level of art because, just as a skilled artist creates a powerful piece of work, an artful relationship-builder creates a circle of people who become their collaborators in achieving success. This is no less a powerful piece of work than a masterpiece that takes the skill, time, tools and materials of an artist to create.

Once you understand *the real meaning* behind networking, everything falls into place. You understand why knowing the rules of networking, which we're talking about in this book, makes such a big difference in how easy it can feel to build relationships and how effective they will become.

But, what happens if you misunderstand the point of networking? You start selling yourself. You want to show off, you want to dazzle, you want to come across as impressively as possible. That 'selling yourself' pressure creates anxiety in the one doing the selling, as well as in those listening to him or her. This is the behaviour that's given networking a bad reputation, and why many people can't help but wince upon hearing the term.

It is also the exact opposite of the behaviour that will attract people to you, and make others want to learn more about you, stay in touch and collaborate. Conversely, non-stop talking about your achievements, or pushing on with a sales pitch, are guaranteed to be a repellent. Talking *at* someone or engaging in duelling monologues, aimed at scoring an imaginary point in the one-upmanship contest of who's more successful, screams 'competition!' rather than collaboration.

But there is one piece in your networker's toolbox that will immediately show that you're serious about building real, authentic relationships. That tool is *interest in others*.

Dr Ivan Misner, the Founder of BNI, who we talked about earlier, once said: "A good networker is like a good talk show interviewer. A good networker asks the guests questions and gives them time to elaborate and respond. I think a good networker is very similar – they ask questions, then listen and let people talk."[43]

At this stage in my personal journey as a networker, one thing has become abundantly clear: the more skilled a person is in connecting with others, the more interest they pay to the person in front of them.

I will never forget an event I attended where the explorer and writer Sir Ranulph Fiennes was a speaker.

Sir Ranulph served with the British Army, including a period of counter-insurgency work while attached to the Army of the Sultanate of Oman. He later undertook numerous expeditions and was the first person to visit both the North and South Poles by surface means, and the first to completely cross Antarctica on foot. Sir Ranulph famously cut off the tips of his own frostbitten fingers with a saw, following the damage that he sustained to his hand while attempting to walk solo and unsupported to the North Pole at age 56. After suffering a massive heart attack and undergoing double coronary artery bypass surgery, at the age of 59 he completed seven marathons in seven days on seven continents, and at 65 he climbed to the summit of Mount Everest. In short, he is one of the world's greatest living explorers. Speaking at the event, Sir Ranulph was full of self-deprecating humour, whilst the audience were awestruck.

Later, I was full of silent wonderment standing in the book-signing queue. When my turn came, Sir Ranulph asked who the book should be dedicated to. "My young daughter," I responded, giving her name. Sir Ranulph looked at me with interest, and asked how old she was. He went on to ask a few other questions, listening carefully to the answers, as if it was I who was the highlight of the night. Taken aback, I couldn't help but be amazed by his curiosity. Having been to all corners of the world, that remarkable man had the kind of humility that can make a fan feel like the main event.

Sir Ranulph taught me one of the most important lessons in my career as a networker: be interested in others and remain curious about their stories.

Lyuba Galkina, one of the best-known names in the vast Russian expat community of 'Londongrad,' is a marketing consultant. She was a senior marketing director at Nike's European Headquarters, a Vice President at Pepsi Russia, and is a co-founder and editor of ZIMA magazine, and a trustee of the Gift of Life charity. She is not merely an acquaintance of, but seems to have close personal friendships with, prominent artists, dancers, actors, film directors, chefs, restauranteurs, journalists, authors and musicians. Lyuba has been instrumental in developing a network of Russian-speaking start-up founders in the UK, and is the bundle of energy behind a charity that has helped hundreds of children with cancer in Russia receive life-saving treatments. She is one of the most impressively well-networked people I know. And so, I was incredibly intrigued to find out which of her personal qualities she credits with making the biggest difference in becoming good at networking.

Her answer? Curiosity! "I think that my natural curiosity, openness and willingness to help make a difference in my personal and professional networking," she told me. And knowing the heights of her achievements as a networker, I believe there is truly no better example of the power of curiosity than Lyuba's journey.

I have asked the same question of numerous other master networkers I've had the fortune to be connected with. Without exception, they've cited their curiosity in others as the key to being good at relationship building. "I am interested in people, I am happy to chat with people and I am interested in what they have to say," summed up one of them.

In his book, *The Attention Switch*,[44] Itzik Amiel, a lawyer, inspirational speaker and founder of Power Networking Academy, coined the term 'Attentional Networking.' He explains that it "demands a totally different set of skills – being a caring, thoughtful, empathic and sympathetic human being. It's all about giving attention to others rather than trying to get attention from them. It's a style of networking that brings amazing results in a much shorter time."[45]

I cannot help but agree with Itzik. Living the modern life of constant busyness, time becomes our most valuable commodity. When someone matters to us, we give him or her our attention and dedicate our time to them. This is to the detriment of many other competing priorities in our life, so the person on the receiving end knows that they are important to you. It is evident that you're sacrificing everything else you could be doing at that moment. Being interested in another person, and giving them your undivided attention, is a powerful thing in interpersonal relationships. Without developing this skill, it is practically impossible to have a strong, authentic connection to another human being.

How does one best show that? How do you pay attention, remain curious and express genuine interest in another person? You do it through listening.

Many of us think that we know how to listen well (at least in theory). We have learned the essentials of not interrupting, matching facial expressions to the topic, and trying to stay on top of what the other person is saying, at least to that point where we can repeat the gist of it. However, in 2016, Jack Zenger and Joseph Folkman of Zenger/Folkman, a leadership development consultancy, published an article in *Harvard Business Review* where they de-mythicized what it means to be a good listener.[46] Their research pointed to what separates an average listener from a really effective one.

As you practice connecting with people, you will notice that masterful listening has a certain magic to it. Those who are skilled at listening tap into the fundamental human need to be understood. And then, once others experience how it feels *to be understood*, they want to be around the listener who possesses that magic... who understands them.

Here are three strategies to adopt, as inspired by the Zenger/Folkman research:

- Great listening is *not* about meaningful nodding when another person is talking, but about having an active conversation. The most effective listeners are those who periodically ask questions that promote discovery and insight. "Asking a good question tells the speaker the listener has not only heard what was said," the research found, "but that they comprehended it well enough to want additional information."[47]

- Good listening is never about being competitive. One-upmanship really is as ineffective as you thought it might be! Instead, it is about cooperation. Whilst you could disagree with what the other person is saying, don't use a conversation as a platform for a debate. The crucial difference is that the person being listened to should feel like the listener is trying to help and not looking for an argument.

- Aim for the conversation to leave a good aftertaste. Great listeners promote a positive interaction that builds the other person's self-esteem. It may just be a short introductory chat at a networking event, but have the other person walk away thinking they've had a very pleasant exchange, and not that you are the cleverest person on Earth, who has made them feel terribly inferior.

I love a metaphor that Zenger and Folkman used, which perfectly describes what great listening is all about:

"While many of us have thought of being a good listener being like a sponge that accurately absorbs what the other person is saying, instead, what these findings show is that good listeners are like trampolines. They are someone you can bounce ideas off of – and rather than absorbing your ideas and energy, they amplify, energize, and clarify your thinking. They make you feel better not merely passively absorbing, but by actively supporting. This lets you gain energy and height, just like someone jumping on a trampoline."[48]

16

BEING VULNERABLE IN ORDER TO BE CONNECTED

When I asked Phillip Journeaux, one of my partners at De Pinna LLP, what personal quality he credits with his development as a successful networker, his response was this: "Empathy. Without understanding what drives and motivates people, it is hard to build meaningful relationships. Listening to and understanding others is key."

This struck a chord with me. Empathy is the golden quality of anyone who is looking to learn to connect with others and build fulfilling and productive relationships. It is the ability to *understand* what the other person might be feeling, and to see a situation from their point of view. It is the alpha and the omega of any connection with another human being: the proverbial quality of putting yourself is someone else's shoes and trying to walk in them.

However, empathy can only be developed through having the courage to be vulnerable. This is because without vulnerability, we cannot access experiences of our own that evoke sympathy and understanding within us. Without having the courage to be vulnerable, we cannot share personal moments with others in a genuine way.

Being vulnerable is the psychological equivalent of being naked. We drop our defences, exposing ourselves to all sorts of elements – rain, wind and sunshine. This is, undoubtedly, a scary prospect. Brené Brown, the researcher on shame and vulnerability I talked about earlier, uses what she calls a vulnerability prayer: "Give me the courage to show up and let myself be seen."[49]

If we feel overwhelmed by the hurt of not having our needs met, perhaps by being ignored or rejected in childhood or early adulthood, when we're at our most helpless, we develop certain defences. These coping mechanisms play an important role when we are powerless, but as empowered adults we come to accept a series of new rules. These rules say that in order to grow, we must be able to tolerate a certain amount of discomfort, and frustration, and the anxiety of being 'in the wrong place at the wrong time.' The pain of being rejected – even the vague prospect of rejection – is shared by the vast majority of people. This is, indeed, quintessentially human.

Our willingness to be vulnerable is actually the fertile soil that's needed for building connections with others. When you become unguarded, others sense that you have nothing to hide, and that leads to an immediate desire to trust. Contrary to popular belief, being self-protective and guarded does not create power over others; it takes away from it. When we engage in a conversation where we feel 'instructed' by an authority figure, the interaction is unlikely to have a profound effect on us. We might follow prescribed directions, but we would not seek a connection or personal relationship with that person. Rationally, we would think that we do not find this company comfortable, but subconsciously we would know that such guarded forcefulness comes from a place of fear.

The fear to let go and be vulnerable, to be wrong, to be imperfect, to be 'only human,' often appears as the need to ensure high standards to the detriment of everything else.

Such people are often too fearful to have spontaneous conversations; their interactions appear forced and lacking fluidity. The irony is that they often crave close social connections, yet the fear to lower one's defences and be vulnerable, to let themselves *be seen*, hinders the development of authentic relationships.

When developing a conversation with a person you're only just getting to know, it is important to keep your defences in place. It is fine to avoid raising certain sensitive subjects, to be cautious about showing too much of yourself, at first. However, the fundamental principle to understand is that you *will* have to come out of your comfort zone. You *should expect* to be vulnerable, to dig deep in order to demonstrate your empathy. You will need to work your 'soul muscle' to try to put yourself in another person's shoes.

It doesn't really matter whether you're discussing the morning session on corporate law or chatting in the queue for afternoon coffee, preparedness to speak to the other person as a fellow human being – imperfect, flawed yet infinitely fascinating – is an absolute must. This will set you head and shoulders above anyone else, and will put you on the path to work one of the most important qualities for any networker: empathy.

17

GETTING OVER THE AWKWARD AND THE SCARY:

THE LESS-PRETTY FACES OF NETWORKING AND THE POWER OF THE FEAR OF REJECTION

Networking is the art of relationship building, pure and simple. Practice it well, and you have a key to open doors that will remain closed for others who haven't realized the real meaning of networking.

Yet, for all the beauty that successful networking carries, there are plenty of fears to combat and challenges to overcome. But this is okay. The simple recognition that building relationships is not easy sailing, that dealing with panic-inducing situations requires hard work, and that people are not always patient, kind and welcoming, is a leap forwards.

Expect difficulties. Know that there are hurdles ahead. There will be anxious moments. But you will survive these. In fact, once you get a handle on mastering them, and brushing off that which doesn't really matter in the scheme of things, you will thrive!

I am speaking with absolute confidence, as one who once froze at the prospect of simply saying my name in front of a dozen of people.

When writing this book, I wanted not only to uncover the joy of relationship-building, but also to be honest about the awkwardness, the strains and the pain that come with it. Think of any valuable relationship in your life. Has it had its difficulties? Have you struggled with certain aspects of it at various points in your life? I am sure that the answer is yes, and if so, you will understand why networking can also be uncomfortable, tricky and more than a little thorny.

First up is that well-known frenemy: the generic fear of entering the room/speaking up/being there. I know it well. The heart palpitations; the sweaty palms; the flushed cheeks. I used to be downright terrified the moment I started experiencing these symptoms. As I found that I was feelings these things at every event I attended, I started wondering whether my 'fear' was in fact the result of panicking about being in front of people, or whether having the physical reaction became my cue to starting getting nervous.

I decided to check this by telling myself that what I'd always thought was debilitating fear was merely the *excitement* of doing something that I cared about. Wasn't it actually excitement – reflected in an accelerated pulse rate and flushed cheeks – that would always come on when I was interacting with people? Perhaps it was not because I was fearful of the interaction, but because I was thrilled and exhilarated!

In effect, I was *choosing* my interpretation of the physical symptoms. I was not overcome with dread; I was in fact stirred, enlivened and electrified! It turns out that the physical symptoms associated with terror and elation are the same, so the secret is to choose your interpretation. This is the time to move away from being consumed by fear and become pumped up with passion. Go with the adrenaline flow.

Secondly, let's face the facts: any relationship is a two-way street. This is a critical point to incorporate into your thinking as you develop your art of networking. This point is both quite elementary and very difficult to genuinely comprehend.

If you are anything like me – an ambitious, achievement-focussed, goal-orientated person – you might want to work on establishing a connection with every interesting person you come across on a networking circuit. Work at it... although it won't always be possible.

There are various reasons for this, but they ultimately boil down to two factors: you do not have enough in common right now, and won't in the foreseeable future... and/or one of the parties does not match the other's interest in connecting.

The latter can be difficult to swallow. We, as human beings, are shaped to care about other people *caring to connect with us*. We talked about this is Chapters 6 and 8: being rejected hurts us on a profoundly deep level. It goes against everything that we, as a species, have evolved to be – social, led by friendly connections, supported by our tribe, part of something bigger.

Being rejected can fundamentally impact our sense of self-worth. Social rejection can make us question our connection to others, our value in the social structure we've chosen to be a part of and, frankly, our place in this world.

Rejection in the context of the professional world can feel like a double blow. But if you've ever felt awful about being spurned in a networking scenario, rest assured that you are not alone. It is meant to feel awful. In fact, it is a sign that you are a socially aware individual and you care about how you're perceived by others. That's great news for anyone working on their relationship-building skills. This is because caring about how you are perceived can be developed into a real drive to cultivate authentic, sustainable business connections that are of mutual benefit. But – and this is a big 'but' – you can only turn it to your advantage if you do not allow the fear to be the decision-maker.

With a hand on my heart I can say that after much work at it, I got to a point where I was able to quash the fear of rejection in a professional networking setting. That's not to say that I don't feel the sting of being rejected, or that I enjoy standing next to someone who expresses no interest in me. It's merely that I have accepted that there will always be those who commit the deadly sins of bad networking, and I have no interest in being in their company. I no longer fear that anyone's rejection will make me see myself as a less-competent professional or an inherently lesser person. I am convinced that rejection is 100% about the other's personal agenda – or their personal flaws – and no reflection of how worthy I am. Of course, it may well be that at a given time my interests do not gel with another's and there is, therefore, little basis for a relationship, despite the effort. And this really is okay.

Relationships are a two-way street, so *you* decide whether you want to engage with those who do not make you feel recognized and secure in their company. Here is a run-down of some of those shady characters who give networking a bad name:

- **The Monopolizer** likes to own another person's time and space. You feel enclosed by them and find it difficult to leave a conversation tactfully, no matter how you try. There may be many reasons behind the monopolizing behaviour, but the outcome is always predictable: it is impossible to build a mutually beneficial relationship with someone who imposes themself on you.

- **The Attention-seeker** rather enjoys being in the spotlight. They are often the heart and soul of any party, but in the context of networking their penchant for being in the limelight means they don't allow another person to open up. As entertaining as the attention-seeker may be, they are often ineffective networkers.

- **The Over-the-shoulder-glancer** is famous for exactly that: peering over your shoulder in search of someone more interesting to talk to. At least is seems that way! There are few things more off-putting than feeling that you aren't worthy of someone's full attention. In fact, this is exactly what Chapter 15 was all about.

It is hard to imagine that many people would want to invest in building a connection with someone who literally keeps overlooking them.

- **The Social-butterfly-on-speed** is a character who's close to my heart. I have been described as a social butterfly, which, while seemingly handy in networking, does come with its challenges. In networking settings there is often an unspoken expectation that we do not engage too deeply in introductory conversations, so it is acceptable (often desirable) to keep things fairly light and move on to meet someone else after ten minutes or so. However, for the first connection to be full of potential, there should be an emphasis on genuine attention and authentic interest in another person. Throwing a business card at someone, or asking to connect on social media two minutes into a conversation – followed by a move sideways to speak to someone else – screams 'shallow.' Such initial chat is unlikely to lead to any mutually beneficial connection.

- **The Ghoster** is not just a detestable character from the world of dating, they're also plentiful on the networking scene. Ghosting – suddenly cutting off communication with someone without explanation, and ignoring attempts to reconnect – is as inconsiderate as you can get. You may have enjoyed talking to someone, sensed a connection and sent a follow-up message suggesting a meeting... and never heard back from them. This is a reflection of narcissism, self-obsession and general lack of concern for others. It's easy to blame yourself: they seemed so professional. But don't do yourself a disservice. Let it go and move on.

Anyone who's serious about building authentic relationships needs to follow the basic rules of disengagement. It is just as important to round off wisely, and ultimately end any conversation – good, bad or otherwise – appropriately. We will talk next about the fine art of ending a conversation, and look later at the strategy and tactics behind a good follow-up.

HOW TO END A CONVERSATION GRACEFULLY

"Everyone can rest assured that very few people are hurt when a conversation ends," says Alison Wood Brooks, a Harvard Business School professor who teaches a class on improving conversation.[50]

This is an important notion, as many think that ending a conversation is a sure sign that they didn't enjoy it in the first place. This isn't necessarily true. Like a good book, any discussion has a beginning, a middle and an end. Honestly, you would not want even the most wonderfully engrossing book to *never end*!

It is fascinating, then, that the authors of a pair of studies published in 2021 – just in time for the cautious easing of the latest round of pandemic social restrictions – concluded the following:

"Conversations almost never ended when both conversants wanted them to and rarely ended when even one conversant wanted them to, and the average discrepancy between desired and actual durations was [sic] roughly half the duration of the conversation. Conversants had little idea when their partners wanted to end and underestimated how discrepant their partners' desires were from their own. These studies suggest that ending conversations is a classic 'coordination problem' that humans are unable to solve because doing so requires information that they normally keep from each other. As a result, most conversations appear to end when no one wants them to."[51]

This is a sobering insight into the reality of our interpersonal communication. First, the conclusion of these studies seems unequivocal about our general lack of awareness of when the end point is suitable and welcome. Secondly, and as a direct result of that lack of awareness, many of us find ourselves stuck in a conversation that extends well past its sell-by date.

When and how to end a conversation is a familiar conundrum for anyone who speaks with others on a regular basis. Although we may be reluctant to pull the plug, we can, in fact, end an interaction in an honest, polite way.

Most of the experienced networkers I've asked about this agreed that it can and must be done... in the right way. We've all cited the need to replenish our glass or our plate, alluded to the call of nature or faked a pressing text message from a client. I will be the first to admit that I have done all of these, and more, to get out of conversations that went on for too long!

In this era of virtual conversations, the likes of Zoom and Teams have offered a vast array of excuses to jump off a call without the need to divulge the real reason. A poor connection, a conflicting diary entry or a home schooling problem to attend to – I suspect many of you are nodding in recognition. Yet, many of us would likely support the idea of being both honest and clear about the reasons for ending a conversation.

Remember, as with any good story, the ending should be just as satisfying as the meaty middle. Even the best of conversations need to end well and clearly. This is welcome, polite and entirely expected.

How about trying something like this:

> "We're here to meet different people, but I've really enjoyed our conversation and would love an opportunity to continue it; so here are my details. Let's arrange a meeting next week over a cup of coffee." (Or, over lunch, drinks, dinner or a virtual call.)

Honesty, of course, is a virtue. And in the context of building authentic relationships with people with whom our connections are genuine, we have to be guided by our actual desire to forge that bond. So, if after the initial interaction you don't feel inclined to take it to the next level, you could also try something along these lines:

> "It was great meeting you, but I don't want to monopolize your time. Let's exchange details so we have a chance to keep in touch in the future."

There will be situations where neither of these scenarios seems apt. And this is the chance for you to be creative and compile your own mental set of 'endings' that fit your personality, various circumstances and your enthusiasm (or lack thereof) for following up.

Do not be afraid to experiment and find the right fit for you.

What is important to remember is that the end of a conversation is its integral part, and becoming adept at it is just as important as getting good at breaking the ice. Take ownership of the good ending and do not leave it to chance.

19

THE ART AND
THE LESSONS
OF VIRTUAL
NETWORKING

My first virtual networking experience was in the spring of 2020, shortly after the initial pandemic-driven shutdown of all in-person events. It was a real eye-opener.

After 'attending' a webinar, I got catapulted into a 'breakout room,' where my avatar was placed around a virtual table next to the cartoon-character likenesses of other participants. Suddenly, somewhat curious and somewhat confused, I found myself as a talking head in the one of the little squares on the screen. My turn to introduce myself came, and I haltingly delivered my elevator pitch. To say that I was out of my comfort zone would be an understatement. I felt like a character in a computer game, a shell of myself, no more than a poorly rendered screen image and a badge.

The other talking heads proceeded to exchange their views on the preceding webinar. There was plenty of inadvertent talking over one another, speaking while muted and family members sticking their heads into the doorway – all the usual pitfalls we've come to recognize in virtual meetings. And while constant interruptions to the flow of conversation won't necessarily kill the vibe in a traditional, face-to-face meeting, in this online setting it was nearly fatal. Frankly, I could not wait to be done with it as quickly as possible. (Yes, I know there's always the excuse of a dropped connection – 'Oops!' – but I am not a quitter.)

It may not have been love at first sight, but virtual networking is clearly here to stay. Even with the much-awaited return of real, live events, online networking offers something that in-person interaction never will:

universal access. Simply put, it does not matter whether you are in London, Lisbon or Lagos... you're only a click away from the chance to connect with others. As much as I love meeting people face-to-face, I cannot help getting excited about expanding my circle of professional and personal connections beyond the geographical location of an old-school conference hall.

Furthermore, for those of us who are now working from home for all or a part of their working week, our digital connections are becoming more and more important. According to Hoyin Cheung, CEO of Remo, one of the pioneering online interactive events platforms, "It has been said that people who make an effort to improve their network are almost 75% more likely to earn a promotion."[52] Therefore, even after work modes have (hopefully, one day!) reset following an almost exclusively work-from-home period, we're still going to see plenty of demand for virtual networking. To illustrate this, OpenExchange, a platform for virtual and hybrid events for companies and investors, expected to run 200,000 of them in 2021, up from 4,000 in 2019.[53]

That first disappointing experience I've described made me rethink my approach to online networking. I realized that, in order to stand a chance of forming bona fide connections in the digital realm, two things are particularly crucial: preparation and the elevator pitch.

Preparation becomes the factor that differentiates a successful, collaborative meeting – where genuine connections are formed – from a completely forgettable exercise, where you're nothing more than a miniscule head and shoulders on someone's laptop.

Virtual networking is a purpose-led activity, where non-verbal language and sparkling personalities play a lesser role, if any at all. You cannot really rely on well-practiced, ice-melting small talk or deep, engaging conversations. You need to know why you are in the room, quite literally. In practice, this calls for carefully researching those who will attend. As we said earlier, asking for a list of participants in advance will be helpful. Look at who the attendees represent, their job description, and anything you can glean on their background and experience. Personally, I stay away from sending a connection request on social media to anyone before the event; this could signal that you're looking for a shortcut to more meaningful connections. But, by all means, use social media to learn more about everyone and make a list of who you'd most like to meet. I prefer creating a short list and a long list, corresponding to my top networking targets and second-tier prospects.

The obvious benefit of such an approach is that, once you are logged on, you can make a beeline for the person who is number one of your to-meet list, before looking for number two, and so on. Do not be shy about being purpose-led. In the context of virtual networking, targeting specific people or companies, or gravitating to discussions on certain topics, shows that you've done your homework.

The truth is, virtual networking is *not* the same as face-to-face networking, and those who know what they're looking for in online meetings will be rewarded with the really valuable contacts and relationships.

At the same time, the elevator pitch takes on a new dimension in digital networking. We talked in Chapter 9 about the need for a tight, informative, attention-grabbing opener that aligns with your purpose. In online networking, the significance of a good elevator pitch increases tenfold. Because you're largely unable to use body language and other non-verbal communication, the straight-up verbal element really does come to the fore.

In virtual networking, your goal is to deliver a condensed, focussed version of your professional role and your purpose. Most of us have a limited attention span when it comes to digesting information transmitted through a digital connection, and the key to making an efficient introduction under those circumstances is having a thoroughly thought-out self-presentation.

Virtual networking may sound somewhat detached, yet the trick is to remember that behind every poorly-lit face and tinny voice in a little digital box there is a flesh-and-blood human being. And so, it follows that behind every online networking encounter there's the potential for a life-changing relationship. Leading with these images of real people, endeavouring to connect at a deep, meaningful level, is the secret to making online relationship-building events work for you.

PART 3

REAP JOY AND MUTUAL BENEFITS FROM BEING CONNECTED

THIS RELATIONSHIP IS A MARATHON, NOT A SPRINT

Over the course of this book, my purpose has been to dispel the myth that networking is a transaction with the single goal of achieving the 'right' connections, which will miraculously propel your career forwards. Not true! It's so much more than that. Networking is, quite simply, a way of life. It's how we humans are meant to live, from an evolutionary perspective.

Once we understand and accept this notion, it is easy to see why the follow-up is so important. As we have learned, the approach to building professional relations is no different from how you approach any other relationship. There is the initial connection stage, the process of getting to know each other, and then the deepening of the relationship. With any one of these missing, there is no relationship to speak of.

Perhaps you meet someone at an event who seems interesting and appears to have a purpose that's similar to yours. You engage in conversation, it goes well, and you decide you'd like to stay in touch as the meeting draws to a close. How do you ensure that the magic of that initial connection is not lost?

As we've said, it's all about seeing relationships you build though networking as marathons, not sprints. If you have ever completed a long-distance race, or any other endurance event that requires mental and physical preparation, careful execution and dogged determination, you know that it pays to know the rules. Similarly, I have three rules that help guide me through the networking process.

First up: exchanging details. I agree, it sounds incredibly basic. What can be simpler than remembering to give your contact info to someone you've just met, and to ask for theirs? The reasons for this are obvious enough – we're concentrating so much on remembering the other person's name, what to say next, how to position ourselves and how to finish the conversation elegantly that, by the time you go your separate ways, you're too overwhelmed to mentally file away the details for later recall.

That is where the Marathon Rule No. 1 comes in. Remember to exchange details!

And how do you go about this? Some of us find that carrying around business cards is still the most convenient way. If so, make yours uniquely different. Use good taste when it comes to design, but consider including your photograph, a quote from your favourite author, or use the other side to duplicate the information in a foreign language if this has significance for you. Don't be afraid to show some flare – life would be very boring indeed if we all adhered to conventional, straight-up-the-middle style.

I am aware, of course, that for many people business cards are fast becoming a thing of the past, especially following the pandemic. (Millennials and Gen Zers surely see these wood byproducts as terribly outmoded.) Many people are opting to trust LinkedIn or other professional social networks with their contact information.

If you are among them, make it a ritual to exchange your digital coordinates at the end of a business conversation.

Alternatively, a contact-exchange and relationship-management app like StayTouch can seamlessly swap contact details, and enhanced features allow you to add further information to help make the connection more personal and keep it alive.

By all means, tap into the ever-growing range of options for keeping your contact details in one place and doling them out when necessary, as long as you adhere to Rule No. 1: just do it!

And this brings us to Marathon Rule No. 2: follow up on the initial meeting as quickly as you can.

As with a long-distance race, not doing so would be like sweating through all the training, turning up at the staging area in all the right gear, completing the warm-up, and then... never starting the run. Neglecting to follow up negates all the hard work you've invested in making the initial connection. True, you *might* bump into the person again elsewhere, but there is a high probability you won't. All told, dropping out at this point would amount to a wasted first meeting.

Any networker worth their salt will have his or her own rule on the timeframe and mode of the follow-up. Some insist that it has to be done within three working days of the initial meeting, and by the means you initially used to exchange contact information, be it email, text, LinkedIn mail or an app. Others are happy to give this a week, and to reach out through any reasonable medium. To my mind, there are no hard and fast rules; it varies depending on factors like your keenness to continue the relationship and how busy you are. Because my diary tends to get full quickly, I like to offload my mental to-do list as efficiently as I can, and follow up within a couple of working days of that first meeting. And, I'll pretty much always use the mode we originally used to exchange contact details.

In the follow-up, I normally suggest a plan for taking the relationship further.

This is where Marathon Rule No. 3 comes in: arrange to meet in person (or have a virtual coffee) with your A-list; make a diary note to get in touch within a few months with the B-list; keep an eye on what's going on with your C-list.

Like many others I know, I use this 'ABC' hierarchy to structure and prioritize my contact list. The A-listers are those with whom I had a strong initial connection, and who are likely to help me in achieving my goals. There's strong justification to work hard on deepening the connection and developing the relationships with these individuals. Therefore, you should put the most effort into maintaining those particular relationships.

Having said that, is there a foolproof way of meeting in person? I hear that 'coffee meetings are the new black.'[54] These might include anything from meeting in a café to treating your contact to a cup of great-quality coffee at your office. If the meeting is initiated by you, it will be your responsibility to cover the tab. The beauty of this option, which you are hosting, is that you have a brief, tightly-focussed opportunity to work on building this nascent relationship. You can safely and effectively use all of the ideas you've gained from reading this book; they aren't meant to be limited to the initial connection. These are the tried and tested ways of building and nurturing any relationship.

But what should you do with the relationships that do not quite fit in with your current professional or personal goals? *Never Eat Alone* author Keith Ferrazzi calls them 'the fringe.'[55] This is what selected social media are for! LinkedIn and similar apps aimed at professional use are supremely effective tools for keeping your contacts apprised of where you are, what you're up to and whether exciting new collaborative opportunities might exist. To be clear, a group posting on LinkedIn does not replace a personal follow-up, but it is a good way to make sure that your B- and C-list contacts are kept in the loop, and that you stay on top of what's happening in their lives.

A final thought on the marathon: if you've ever competed in a big race as a novice (I have; 'novice' is my favourite category!), an elite athlete might have gotten ahead of you by a whole lap or more. This is how it might feel when you make a connection with someone you perceived to be out of your league. Remember the common playground principle – just get in there and play! – and feel good about the fact that you struck up the conversation. Granted, it might seem a bit intimidating to invite that important person for a coffee as a follow-up, but you'll often benefit from what's called 'the Benjamin Franklin effect.' This is the cognitive bias that causes people to like someone more after they do that person a favour. Dale Carnegie cited this phenomenon in *How to Win Friends and Influence People*, interpreting the request for a favour – in this case, simply requesting a friendly chat – as "a subtle but effective form of flattery."

Franklin himself described it as an old maxim in his autobiography: "He that has once done you a kindness will be more ready to do you another, than he whom you yourself have obliged."[56]

Let that be encouragement for you to connect with that somewhat intimidating VIP, and then another person and another, whose opinions and advice you value due to their reputation or position. That first move may well mark the start of a productive and mutually beneficial relationship.

21

WISDOM FOR AMBITIOUS NETWORKERS

Networking is a process of self-discovery, no matter how experienced a practitioner you are. Whether you opened this book as a newbie to the world of professional relationship building, are experienced but looking for a more structured approach to networking, or perhaps feel that a more holistic take on the process would help... we all have things to learn!

With that in mind, I reached out to those who I have watched work their magic and build effective and authentic connections with people over the years. Some of the wisdom they've generously shared with me appears throughout this book. Other gems are collected here, in this final chapter that you can dip in and out of, to be motivated and inspired.

Along the way, continually challenge yourself to think differently and always choose the relationship – ahead of selling, impressing and proving someone wrong.

THE BEST ADVICE FOR THOSE WHO ARE JUST STARTING:

"There is a mistaken belief that one has to be in a senior stage of their career to be involved in networking. In my view, networking is a set of skills that should be encouraged and learned as early as possible, so that, by the time part of your job involves the generation of business, you are actually good at networking, which enables you to bring in new business."

ARTEM DOUDKO,
FCIArb, Solicitor-advocate, Partner and
Head of Russia & CIS Disputes, London Dispute
Resolution Practice, Osborne Clarke LLP

ENDURING ADVICE THAT IS USEFUL FOR EVERYONE:

"Relax! Find someone that has been doing this for a while, because there was a time when they didn't do this and they can give you hints and tips. I remember somebody saying to me that if I was at a physical networking event, and did not know anybody, to remember two things, which was to hunt out another like-minded soul, perhaps in the line for tea or coffee, and just go up and say hello.

"If that didn't work, rather than waiting for the ground to open and swallow you up, then you can fake a telephone call, go outside and freshen up, take a deep breath, and go back in and start again. I still use both of those to this day!

"The other pointer that I would give is to forget the idea of selling, and to fight any suggestion that you have to go to a networking event and come back with X number of business cards of Y number of leads. I would rather have one strong connection than ten 30-second conversations, because networking is engagement. Engagement takes time, and it takes time to build relationships. I have made many personal friends through networking. And that is the goal, not selling – business will follow. It is about creating that army of advocates for you and your business (not the other way around) and being an advocate for others in return."

KEVIN ROGERS, Partner and Chairman,
Wilson Browne Solicitors, and President,
Northamptonshire Chamber of Commerce

THE BEST TIME-TESTED TIPS TO KEEP IN YOUR BACK POCKET:

"Try these practical tips and techniques to help you overcome networking nerves:

a. Ideally, go with a friend, have fun and work the room together – those have been my best and most enjoyable networking experiences. Avoid just standing together chatting between the two of you, to the exclusion of others.

b. If you feel a bit overwhelmed when you first walk in, do a lap of the room and see if you see a friendly or interesting person to whom you might introduce yourself.

c. People enjoy being entertained and inspired. Talk about interesting things in your life and the outside world, as well as war stories from your professional life that can be shared without breaking confidences, and which indirectly reflect your knowledge and experience. At all costs, though, avoid a sales pitch.

d. Be kind to others who might feel equally nervous and are similarly looking for an opportunity to chat.

e. Ask if the person you have been chatting with might have a business card, and if they do then offer your own. Follow up with a connection request on LinkedIn shortly after.

f. Don't get drunk. Repeat: do not get drunk, no matter how challenging you might find networking to be. Many hard-won reputations have been lost by drinking too much at a networking event."

CLARE MURRAY, Managing Partner, CM Murray LLP

ON GETTING OUT OF YOUR COMFORT ZONE:

"Find your comfort zone, and then move on from there. Develop your expertise and start talking to people. The worst thing that can happen is that they don't really engage. It's a mere rejection."

HUMPHREY DOUGLAS, Energy Partner, SNR Denton

ON BEING INTERESTED IN PEOPLE:

"In the early days, I just didn't sufficiently understand other peoples' businesses. I came to realize quite soon that you need a basic level of knowledge of what people do, and what their business is all about, in order to understand how you can help them – what you and your firm or organization can add to their business. Then, you can have a conversation that is interesting and useful to them as well, and they can see that you are interested in them, which is a key step in establishing a relationship."

TREVOR BARTON, Consultant to CMS
Cameron McKenna Nabarro Olswang LLP,
and Vice President, Russo-British Chamber of
Commerce Advisory Council

ON THE TRUE MEANING OF NETWORKING:

"[Networking] can mean that 'slippery eels feeling' that you get in your stomach when you walk alone into a room full of strangers for an event, and then the joy and relief of spotting a friendly face you know, which helps you relax and start to enjoy yourself.

"By contrast, networking within a group where you have built up a long-standing, consistent presence and genuine friendships is a wonderful, affirming experience. But, you only get to that stage by feeling the fear of networking time after time, and just doing it anyway.

"Overall, it's about being open to meeting people, listening to their stories and experiences and sharing your own, and building credibility and trust with people. And, it helps if you can be authentic and a little bit entertaining too."

CLARE MURRAY, Managing Partner, CM Murray LLP

THE REAL SPIRIT BEHIND THE TERM:

"Networking is about finding other people that are looking to solve the same problems as you are."

ANITA HOFFMANN, Managing Director, Executiva Limited

ANYTHING IS POSSIBLE:

"Through networking, anything is possible. As with daily interactions of any kind with other individuals, it leads to an endless number of possibilities. As you develop within your selected fields, this becomes acutely clear. Through gaining additional contacts you will be able to call on people to make things happen for yourself and for others. The old adage, 'It's not what you know but who you know' comes to mind, but not in a derogatory way. Knowledge is required and knowledge is power, but where you have gone out of your way to make contacts that can facilitate a business deal or find you that new job, then that is something you have earned and, in my opinion, deserve."

BEN WELLS, Partner, Candey, and Founder and Chairman, RusFor

ENDNOTES

1. Ivan R Misner, Don Morgan, *Masters of Networking: Building Relationships for your Pocketbook and Soul* (Austin: Bard Press, 2000), p.45

2. Kathryn Dill, "Your next boss: more harmony, less authority," *Wall Street Journal*, January 12, 2021, https://www.wsj.com/articles/your-next-boss-may-be-more-of-a-coach-than-a-dictator-11610467280

3. "Homepage," Merriam-Webster dictionary online, last accessed January 28, 2022, https://www.merriam-webster.com

4. Ibid.

5. Oxford English Dictionary online, accessed January 31, 2022, https://www.oxfordlearnersdictionaries.com/definition/english/networking

6. Hilary Gallo, *The Power of Soft: How to get what you want without being a ****** (London: Unbound, 2016), p.115

7. Keith Ferrazzi, Tahl Raz, *Never Eat Alone, Expanded and Updated... And other secrets of success, one relationship at a time* (London: Portfolio Penguin, 2014), p.62–63

8. "It might seem crazy," *The Economist*, March 20, 2021, p.50

9. Dale Carnegie, *How to Win Friends and Influence People* (London: Vermilion, 2006), p.104

10. Emily Torres, "The Good Trade," accessed on November 13, 2021, https://www.thegoodtrade.com/features/taking-yourself-too-seriously

11. Keith Ferrazzi, Tahl Raz, *Never Eat Alone, Expanded and Updated... And other secrets of success, one relationship at a time* (London: Portfolio, Penguin, 2014), p.251

12. The Harvard Study of Adult Development, accessed January 31, 2022, https://www.adultdevelopmentstudy.org

13. Liz Mineo, *"Good genes are nice, but joy is better,"* The Harvard Gazette, April 11, 2017, https://news.harvard.edu/gazette/story/2017/04/over-nearly-80-years-harvard-study-has-been-showing-how-to-live-a-healthy-and-happy-life/

14. Ibid.

15. Rutger Bregman, trans. Elizabeth Manton and Erica Moore, *Humankind: A Hopeful History* (Bloomsbury Publishing, 3rd edition 2021), p.62–67

16. Ibid.

17. "He was known as Tom Terrific," *The Glory of Baseball*, September 3, 2020, https://www.thegloryofbaseball.org/new-blog-1/2020/9/3/he-was-known-as-tom-terrific

18. "Establishing the cause of death," *The Economist*, July 31, 2021, p.58

19. "Most popular social networks worldwide as of July 2021, ranked by number of active users," accessed November 2021, https://www.statista.com/statistics/272014/global-social-networks-ranked-by-number-of-users/

20. Jon Yates, *Fractured: Why Our Societies are Coming Apart and How We Put Them Back Together Again* (Manchester: Harper North, 2021), p.103

21. Ibid.

22. Brené Brown, *Daring Greatly: How the Courage to be Vulnerable Transforms the Way We Live, Love, Parent and Lead* (London: Penguin Life, 2015), p.176

23. Ibid.

24. Christopher Kukk, "Survival of the Fittest Has Evolved: Try Survival of the Kindest," *NBC News*, March 8, 2017, https://www.nbcnews.com/better/relationships/survival-fittest-has-evolved-try-survival-kindest-n730196

25. Brigette Tasha Hyacinth, *Leading the Workforce of the Future: Inspiring a Mindset of Passion, Innovation and Growth* (MBA Caribbean Organisation, 2020), p.16

26. Kathy Caprino, "Three Simple Steps To Identify Your Life Purpose And Leverage It In Your Career," *Forbes*, November 28, 2018, https://www.forbes.com/sites/kathycaprino/2018/11/28/three-simple-steps-to-identify-your-life-purpose-and-leverage-it-in-your-career/?sh=24171397695f

27. Team Tony, "How to find your purpose," *Tony Robbins*, accessed August 27, 2021, https://www.tonyrobbins.com/stories/date-with-destiny/what-is-my-purpose/

28. Dan Stern, "What the Top 3% of Harvard MBA's Did To Become Rich – That You Can Do Too," citing Mark McCormack, *What They Don't Teach You at Harvard Business School: Notes from a Street-Smart Executive* (New York: Bantam, 1986), who was referring to the 1979 study of Harvard MBA students, *LinkedIn*, November 11, 2015, https://www.linkedin.com/pulse/what-top-3-harvard-mbas-did-become-rich-you-can-do-too-dan-stern

29. Patricia Lajara de Camilleri, "Why helping others drives our success," LinkedIn, January 26, 2021, https://www.linkedin.com/pulse/why-helping-others-drives-our-success-patricia-lajara-de-camilleri

30. Adam Grant, *Give and Take: Why Helping Others Drives our Success* (London: Penguin Books, 2014)

31. Ivan Misner, PhD, "Givers Gain® is Transformational," *BNI.com*, November 20, 2020, https://www.bni.com/the-latest/blog-news/givers-gain-is-transformational

32. Michael Gervais, "How to Stop Worrying About What Other People Think of You," *Harvard Business Review*, May 2, 2019, https://hbr.org/2019/05/how-to-stop-worrying-about-what-other-people-think-of-you

33. "Extraversion or Introversion," The Myers & Briggs Foundation, accessed September 2021, https://www.myersbriggs.org/my-mbti-personality-type/mbti-basics/extraversion-or-introversion.htm?bhcp=1

34. Meghan Holohan, "Winning Personality: The advantages of being an ambivert," *Today*, February 8, 2016, https://www.today.com/health/winning-personality-advantages-being-ambivert-t70236

35. Adam Grant, "Rethinking the Extroverted Sales Ideal: The Ambivert Advantage," The Wharton School, University of Pennsylvania, 2013, accessed on September 12, 2021, https://faculty.wharton.upenn.edu/wp-content/uploads/2013/06/Grant_PsychScience2013.pdf

36. Dale Carnegie, *How to Win Friends and Influence People* (London: Vermilion, 2006), p.87

37. The term was coined in 1923 by Bronisław Kasper Malinowski, "The Problem of Meaning in Primitive Languages" in: Charles Kay Ogden and Ivor Armstrong Richards, *The Meaning of Meaning: A Study of the Influence of Language upon Thought and of the Science of Symbolism* (New York: Harcourt, Brace & World, Inc., 293–336), accessed on September 27, 2021, http://jeesusjalutasallveelaeval.blogspot.com/2017/09/phatic-communion.html

38. Emma Yeomans, "Chitchat 101: BPP University Law School offers lessons in small talk," *The Times*, February 16, 2021, https://www.thetimes.co.uk/article/chitchat-101-bpp-university-law-school-offers-lessons-in-small-talk-2jnnhlcpk

39. Michael Kardas, Amit Kumar, and Nicholas Epley, "Overly Shallow? Miscalibrated Expectations Create a Barrier to Deeper Conversation," *Journal of Personality and Social Psychology*, September 30, 2021, https://www.apa.org/pubs/journals/releases/psp-pspa0000281.pdf

40. Ibid.

41. Ibid.

42. Ibid.

43. Ivan Misner, "Don't Show Off, Show Interest," *IvanMisner.com*, September 20, 2021, https://ivanmisner.com/dont-show-off-show-interest/?utm_source=rss&utm_medium=rss&utm_campaign=dont-show-off-show-interest

44. Itzik Amiel, *The Attention Switch* (Croydon, Surrey: Filament Publishing, 2014)

45. Ibid.

46. Jack Zenger and Joseph Folkman, "What Great Listeners Actually Do," *Harvard Business Review*, July 14, 2016, https://hbr.org/2016/07/what-great-listeners-actually-do

47. Ibid.

48. Ibid.

49. Brené Brown, *Daring Greatly: How the Courage to be Vulnerable Transforms the Way We Live, Love, Parent and Lead* (London: Penguin Life, 2015), p.42

50. As quoted in: Joe Pinsker, "How to End a Conversation Without Making Up an Excuse," *The Atlantic*, March 18, 2021, https://www.theatlantic.com/family/archive/2021/03/conversations-never-end/618309/

51. Adam T. Mastroianni, Daniel T Gilbert, Gus Cooney, and Timothy D Wilson, "Do Conversations End When People Want Them to?" *Psychological and Cognitive Sciences,* Vol 118, No. 10 (March 2021), p.1, https://www.pnas.org/content/pnas/118/10/e2011809118.full.pdf

52. Hoyin Cheung, "Virtual Networking Explained," *Remo.co*, October 22, 2019, https://remo.co/blog/2019/10/22/virtual_networking_explained/

53. "Update your calendar," *The Economist*, September 4, 2021, p.51

54. Simone Andersen, *The Networking Book: 50 ways to develop strategic relationships* (London: LID Publishing Ltd, 2015), p.120

55. Keith Ferrazzi, Tahl Raz, Never Eat Alone, Expanded and Updated...And other secrets of success, one relationship at a time (London: Portfolio, Penguin, 2014), p.219

56. Benjamin Franklin, *The Autobiography of Benjamin Franklin* (London: Macmillan & Co Ltd, 1921), p.48

ABOUT THE AUTHOR

Alisa Grafton is a lawyer, an English scrivener notary and a partner at De Pinna LLP. Originally from Moscow, she began discovering the power of networking when she first joined a traditional firm in the City of London in 2000. She has written and spoken about networking for a number of years, before writing a book based on her practitioner's experience and research. In *Great Networking*, she shares personal lessons, tried and tested secrets of genuine, authentic yet effective networkers, and the way fruitful professional relationships can change the course of your life for the better.

THE BLURB

Relationships are at the heart of everything in life. But whilst we invest a considerable amount of effort into our personal relationships, we often overlook the professional kind. Yet this is the area of our lives where our investment of positive effort will generate significant benefits.

Great Networking is full of candid, personal accounts of the ups and downs faced on the journey to become good at professional relationships, with real-life lessons from those who have developed expertise in connecting with others. Bringing into play social media and the virtual angle, this is a complete, unique guide for soulful professional relationship-building in the 21st century, from a practitioner who has walked the walk and who is sharing what she has learned over a 20-year career in professional services.